C000054022

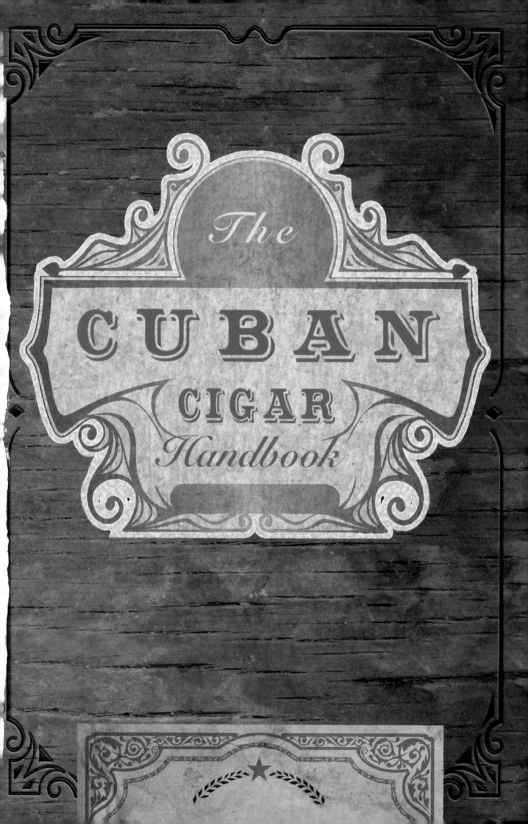

# The

# CUBAN

# (CIGAR)

# Handbook

*The*

# CUBAN
## CIGAR
### *Handbook*

Copyright © 2016 by Appleseed Press Book Publishers, LLC.

First published in Great Britain in 2016 by Souvenir Press Ltd
43 Great Russell Street, London WC1B 3PD

The right of Appleseed Press Book Publishers, LLC to be
identified as the author of this work has been asserted in accordance
with section 77 of the Copyright, Designs and Patents Act, 1988

All rights reserved.
No part of this publication may be reproduced, stored in a
retrieval system or transmitted, in any form or by any means,
electronic, mechanical, photocopying, or otherwise, without
the prior permission of the Copyright owner.

ISBN 9780285643567

Printed and bound in India

# CONTENTS

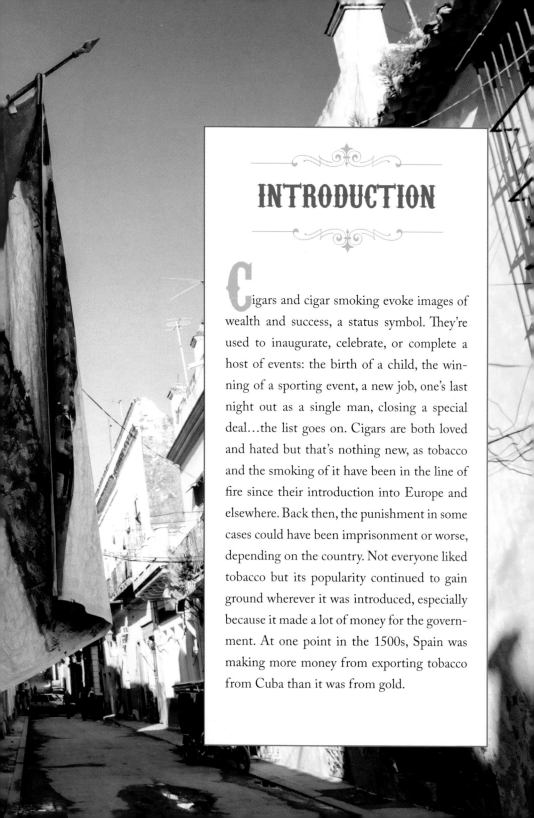

# INTRODUCTION

Cigars and cigar smoking evoke images of wealth and success, a status symbol. They're used to inaugurate, celebrate, or complete a host of events: the birth of a child, the winning of a sporting event, a new job, one's last night out as a single man, closing a special deal…the list goes on. Cigars are both loved and hated but that's nothing new, as tobacco and the smoking of it have been in the line of fire since their introduction into Europe and elsewhere. Back then, the punishment in some cases could have been imprisonment or worse, depending on the country. Not everyone liked tobacco but its popularity continued to gain ground wherever it was introduced, especially because it made a lot of money for the government. At one point in the 1500s, Spain was making more money from exporting tobacco from Cuba than it was from gold.

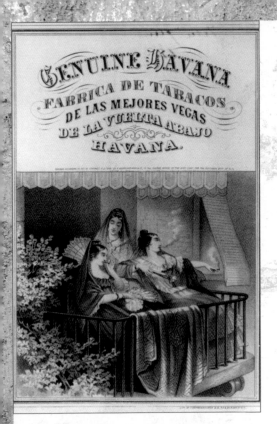

The exact origin of tobacco is unknown and a subject that scientists can't agree on, but it's been narrowed down to the Americas, all the way up to Canada. What is certain is that the first Europeans to discover tobacco and Cuba in 1492 were the same ones who brought it back to Spain. Today we know that it was in use for centuries prior to their discovery. Christopher Columbus and his expedition observed the Taino Indians smoking tobacco through a pipe at ceremonies and it's been documented that they saw the natives smoking something that's described as a primitive modern-day cigar.

It took a while to catch on in Spain and Europe, but tobacco would eventually become the catalyst for colonization in this part of the world. The first tobacco plantations were established in the late 1500s and early 1600s in Cuba, and tobacco production would surpass sugar before the end of the 17th century and support a good part of the population. By the 1800s there would be 5,500 plantations on the island. Tobacco leaf would be sent to the Spanish ports of Cadiz and Cartagena as well as to the cities of Moguer and Seville in Spain and Lisbon in Portugal. Eventually, it spread to the rest of Europe, Russia, and Asia, although in some cases decades later.

For approximately the first century, tobacco leaf sent from the new world would be rolled into cigars in Spain. It would take this long for them to discover that rolled cigars traveled better than loose-leaf. The rolling of cigars in Cuba (Havana) for export began slowly and on a small scale in the late 18th century but would become the norm in the next century, making the tobacco industry a dominant feature on the business landscape.

Although Cuban cigars continued to gain notoriety through the 20th century, there were many ups and downs in the cigar industry in Cuba during the 1900s. The century started off on a dour note with the end of the second War of Independence in 1898. The land and industry, including tobacco, had been decimated almost to the point of no return. Tobacco seed from the original strain had to be imported from Mexico. There was a shift in ownership and direction but the industry persevered and production once again began to climb until the Great Depression of 1929–1939.

The effects of the Depression on the United States are well documented but it didn't end there. Due to the enormous economic connection between the United States and Cuba during this time, cigar sales once again took a hit in Cuba. After all, cigars are not a necessity when you're having difficulty putting food on the table. Prior to the mid 1950s, half of all cigars produced in Cuba went to the United States, as well as two-thirds of tobacco leaf that would mostly be rolled in factories in Florida and New Jersey.

After Fidel Castro's revolution, the industry took another hit, with many people fleeing the country. Women had always been involved in the cigar industry in Cuba but it wasn't until this time in the late 1960s that they were welcomed into the *galera* or rolling room. Before that, the job of rolling cigars was a man's domain. With the shortage

of rollers, Celia Sanchez opened the doors to women working on the rolling floor by opening the El Laguito factory and officially creating the Cohiba brand. Cohibas would be rolled only in this factory and only by women working in the rolling rooms. Today El Laguito still rolls only Cohiba, but you will find both men and women rolling them.

Once again, adjustments were made and tobacco and cigar production returned to previous levels until 1979–1980 when the blue mold destroyed almost all of that year's harvest and most of the next year's harvest. Production levels and the quality of the cigars improved in the late 1980s and early 1990s, coinciding with a resurgence of popularity in cigar smoking. Wanting to take advantage of the new market, there was an over-production of cigars with a decline in quality by the year 2000. With the multinational company Altadis buying a controlling share of Habanos S.A. in 2002, things began to take a turn for the better.

After the revolution in 1962, the tobacco industry was nationalized and the Cuban State created Cubatabaco to handle all things related to tobacco. In 1994, Habanos S.A. was created to handle the sales and in 2001 Tabacuba was created to handle manufacturing.

As with the beginning of the 20th century and after the revolution of 1959, the cigar industry in Cuba is at a crossroad once again. The industry is rebounding back from two horrible years due to weather conditions at the beginning of the decade and experiencing warming relations with the United States, making the prospects of that market a possibility. Will the Cubans be able to handle the increase in production and what will the quality of the cigars be when the possibility becomes a reality?

Most people that light up a cigar don't give much thought beyond the rolling table when it comes to the manufacturing of a cigar but there's a lot more to it than that and it's confusingly different at times in the case of Cuba. There are a few steps before that finished product touches someone's lips. You have the growing, harvesting, and curing of the tobacco leaf on the farms in Pinar del Rio and then the processing of the leaf at the factory.

Tobacco growing season in Cuba starts around mid-October and ends around the end of December. However, this isn't where it all begins. The land is prepared through the summer between June and August, with the growing of seedlings starting in September (taking at least 45 days) until the beginning of November.

There are two types of tobacco grown, shade-grown (*tapado*) used for wrapper and sun-grown used for filler and binder. The plant is made up of three parts: the sun-grown top of the plant is called the *Ligero* (strong and full bodied), the middle is the *Seco* (medium body for aroma) and the bottom part of the plant is the *Volado* (lighter bodied for combustion). The wrapper leaf is the more difficult to produce and garners the most money.

Harvesting tobacco begins sometime in December and finishes into March. From the time you plant to the time you finish picking, it's 16 weeks for sun-grown and 17 weeks for shade-grown. The tobacco plant is not harvested all in one day. Starting from the bottom of the plant, two to three leaves are picked at one time every few days. After the leaves are picked, they're taken to the curing barn, sown in pairs, hung on poles, and placed on racks starting from the bottom, and moving them towards the top as the leaves begin to change color from green to golden brown. The farmer, or tobacco grower, manually controls the temperature and humidity in the barn by constantly monitoring and adjusting the levels by opening and closing windows

EBRERO·MARZO·1941

CARNAVAL

EN LA HABANA

and doors so the air can flow freely through the barn. The process takes about 50 days.

Once the farmer has cured his leaf, he sells it to the state at fixed prices. A farmer can only sell his leaf to the government but only after taking out his allotted amount for personal consumption. Once the state buys the leaf from the farmer it assumes responsibility after that. The leaf is priced according to quality and this is when the leaf is classified and put into designated groups.

Wrappers are sorted by size, texture, and color into more than 50 categories. The leaf will have received its first fermentation in the farmer's barn but here at the warehouse, after being classified, the leaf will be put through another one. After this final fermentation, the leaves are put on racks for airing a few days before being packed in bales for aging for up to two years, depending on the leaf. The bales are marked with information about the leaf within; date of harvest and packaging as well as size and strength of the leaf and specific characteristics for blending. Once all this is done, up to two years later, the carefully marked bales make their way to the various factories across the country, but mostly to Havana.

After all this work, we still don't have a finished product. The leaf is now at the factory; of course there is a steady supply every year to replace the leaf that's being used throughout the year, providing all goes well in the fields. Once the leaf is at the factory it will go through another series of steps before being turned into a cigar and a few more before it enters a box.

**1. La Moja:** Preparing the wrapper leaf, which at this point may be a bit dry. The leaves will be separated and sprayed with a fine mist to add moisture and make them easier to handle. Excess moisture is shaken off so the leaf won't be stained and they're hung on racks so the moisture is absorbed evenly. Once that's done, they will go to the next department for processing. The filler and binder leaves will be removed from their bales and inspected for moisture, adding or removing it, whichever is needed at the time of sorting.

**2. Despalillo:** The stripping department is where the wrapper leaf goes for the removal of the central vein of the leaf, creating two halves. The skilled worker will also grade or organize the leaf in piles according to color, quality, and size. It's generally women that do this job.

**3. La Barajita:** The filler and binder leaf go to the blending department. The leaf is carefully removed from the bales, separated, and put on racks in order to obtain the proper moisture. When the leaf is ready for handling the *ligador* (master blender) puts together the blends for the cigars to be rolled according to the information that was inscribed on the bales. Each roller is given a pile of leaves: wrapper, binder, *seco*, *volado*, and *ligero* and told the combinations and *vitola* (size) he will be rolling that day. There is a specific blend for each cigar to be rolled and the master blender makes sure that it's followed, according to Habanos S.A. and the Regulatory Council. He is the only one in the factory who knows what the blends are for any given cigar. He is given a future production schedule and from that

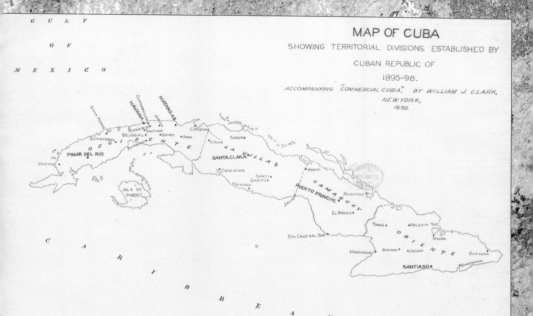

MAP OF CUBA

SHOWING TERRITORIAL DIVISIONS ESTABLISHED BY

CUBAN REPUBLIC OF

1895-98.

ACCOMPANYING "COMMERCIAL CUBA," BY WILLIAM J. CLARK,
NEW YORK,
1898.

list he orders his tobacco from the warehouse in Pinar del Rio.

**4. Galera:** The rolling room where every roller has his own table and tools to perform the day's tasks. Once they are given their assignment they are required to roll a certain quantity for the day, depending on the *vitola*. The average is about 100 cigars for something in the smaller range.

**5. Revisa:** The quality control room is one of a series of moments that the cigars are checked for quality of construction. Here, every cigar is checked one-by-one for imperfections, both by look and feel, and to make sure they meet exact specifications (length and ring gauge). If either the wrapper has flaws or if by squeezing it's felt that it's either too tight or too loose in spots, the cigar is put aside and the roller docked. The boxes the cigars come in are marked with the person who rolled the cigars. If a roller has one or two bad ones in his or her day's work, no problem, but if it's more than that and happens on a daily basis, that roller may need to be demoted.

**6. Escaparate:** The room where the cigars will go after they've been through quality control. Here, they will rest for about a week for humidity conditioning after they've

been fumigated for fungi and insects. Excess humidity will be released before the cigars are sent to the next department.

**7. Escojida:** This is where the cigars go to be laid out on the *Mesa de Seleccion de Colores*, or color sorting table. It's said that there are more than 60 shades of (cigar) brown and there are gifted people called *Escojedores* who are better at distinguishing them than the average person. This process takes place to ensure that the cigars packed in each box are all the same shade or color. At any time during this process the *Escojedor* can discard any cigar, making this another quality control spot check.

**8. Anillado:** This is where the cigars are banded. Prior to coming here, the cigars have already been sorted by shade and boxed best side facing up, without bands. In this department the worker will carefully remove all the cigars and band them according to how they've been boxed before receiving them, that is to say, best side up (facing outwards).

**9. Filetiado:** The trimming department is where the boxes for the cigars are prepared before being stuffed with cigars. The boxes are dressed with the fancy paper coverings that aficionados know so well.

**10. Embalaje:** The packing department is the last stage before the cigars are picked up and taken to the warehouse before shipping. Cigar boxes are put into large cardboard boxes stamped with content information: cigar brand, type, quantity, weight, date, and factory name.

**11. The tasting panel**: I leave this for the end because in the H. Upmann factory it's done every morning for the previous day's work. In this room, about a dozen factory workers from different departments will sit in for a final testing of the day's work. A cross section of cigars from a number of rollers will be tested one more time and rated. Once again, if they don't meet the factory's standards, someone will be reprimanded.

Once the cigars are finally packed in large boxes and stamped with content information they are shipped to a warehouse in Havana and from there they are shipped to locations within Cuba and around the world. Cigars that are rolled in a factory in Cuba are not sold directly from the store connected to that factory, if that factory has one. Each country the cigars are shipped to will have only one importer who in turn will sell the cigars to individual cigar shops within their country.

So there you have it, much more than the average cigar smoker anticipated, that's for sure. As I previously stated, there's a lot more to a cigar than what goes on at the rolling table. The cigar has been witness to many changes both in its perception and within the industry itself, but some things have remained constant. Cuba produces the best tobacco in the world, a perception that has remained constant. Conditions, manufacturing, and construction of the finished product may have changed, but the quality of the tobacco and the soil that it comes from haven't.

Let us try to remember that the next time we light up a Habanos.

— Matteo Speranza

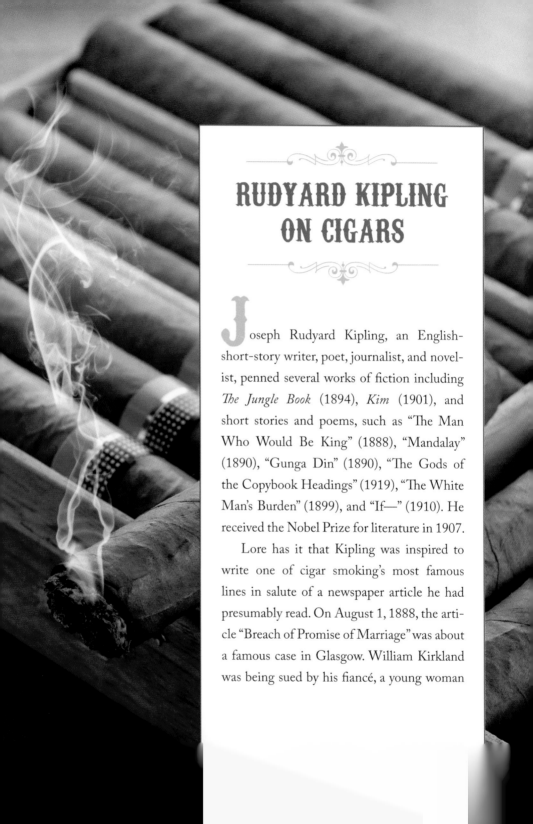

# RUDYARD KIPLING ON CIGARS

Joseph Rudyard Kipling, an English-short-story writer, poet, journalist, and novelist, penned several works of fiction including *The Jungle Book* (1894), *Kim* (1901), and short stories and poems, such as "The Man Who Would Be King" (1888), "Mandalay" (1890), "Gunga Din" (1890), "The Gods of the Copybook Headings" (1919), "The White Man's Burden" (1899), and "If—" (1910). He received the Nobel Prize for literature in 1907.

Lore has it that Kipling was inspired to write one of cigar smoking's most famous lines in salute of a newspaper article he had presumably read. On August 1, 1888, the article "Breach of Promise of Marriage" was about a famous case in Glasgow. William Kirkland was being sued by his fiancé, a young woman named Maggie Watson. Watson had insisted that Kirkland give up cigars upon their marriage, which she considered an unappealing habit. Kirk- land refused the request and the bride. They settled it in court. The following was the inspired result of such marital conflict:

# The Betrothed

"You must choose between me
and your cigar."
*Breach of Promise Case, circa, 1885*

Open the old cigar-box, get me a
Cuba stout,
For things are running crossways,
and Maggie and I are out.

We quarrelled about Havanas—we
fought o'er a good cheroot,
And I know she is exacting, and
she says I am a brute.

Open the old cigar-box—let me
consider a space;
In the soft blue veil of the vapour
musing on Maggie's face.

Maggie is pretty to look at—
Maggie's a loving lass,
But the prettiest cheeks must
wrinkle, the truest of loves must
pass.

There's peace in a Laranaga, there's
calm in a Henry Clay;
But the best cigar in an hour is
finished and thrown away—

Thrown away for another as
perfect and ripe and brown—
But I could not throw away
Maggie for fear o' the talk o' the
town!

Maggie, my wife at fifty—grey and
dour and old—
With never another Maggie to
purchase for love or gold!

And the light of Days that have
Been the dark of the Days that
Are,
And Love's torch stinking and
stale, like the butt of a dead
cigar—

The butt of a dead cigar you are
bound to keep in your pocket—
With never a new one to light
tho' it's charred and black to the
socket!

Open the old cigar-box—let me
consider a while.
Here is a mild Manilla—there is a
wifely smile.

Which is the better portion—
bondage bought with a ring,

Or a harem of dusky beauties fifty
tied in a string?

Counsellors cunning and silent—
comforters true and tried,
And never a one of the fifty to
sneer at a rival bride?

Thought in the early morning,
solace in time of woes,
Peace in the hush of the twilight,
balm ere my eyelids close,

This will the fifty give me, asking
nought in return,
With only a Suttee's passion—to
do their duty and burn.

This will the fifty give me. When
they are spent and dead,
Five times other fifties shall be my
servants instead.
The furrows of far-off Java, the
isles of the Spanish Main,
When they hear my harem is
empty will send me my brides
again.

I will take no heed to their
raiment, nor food for their mouths
withal,
So long as the gulls are nesting, so
long as the showers fall.

I will scent 'em with best vanilla,
with tea will I temper their hides,
And the Moor and the Mormon
shall envy who read of the tale of
my brides.

For Maggie has written a letter to
give me my choice between
The wee little whimpering Love
and the great god Nick o' Teen.

And I have been servant of Love
for barely a twelvemonth clear,
But I have been Priest of Cabanas
a matter of seven year;

And the gloom of my bachelor
days is flecked with the cheery
light
Of stumps that I burned to
Friendship and Pleasure and Work
and Fight.

And I turn my eyes to the future
that Maggie and I must prove,

But the only light on the marshes
is the Will-o'-the-Wisp of Love.

Will it see me safe through my
journey or leave me bogged in the
mire?
Since a puff of tobacco can cloud
it, shall I follow the fitful fire?

Open the old cigar-box—let me
consider anew—
Old friends, and who is Maggie
that I should abandon you?

A million surplus Maggies are
willing to bear the yoke;
And a woman is only a woman,
but a good Cigar is a Smoke.

Light me another Cuba—I hold to
my first-sworn vows.
If Maggie will have no rival, I'll
have no Maggie for Spouse!

# HOTEL NACIONAL DE CUBA (HAVANA)

**A**sk any cigar smoker who travels frequently to Havana what his favorite patio in that city is and he (or she) is most likely to mention the one at the Hotel Nacional. Any trip to Havana with this bunch of people will almost always include at least one visit to the Hotel Nacional (or more) to basically just hang out and have a smoke or two, at any time of day...open 24 hours. I've even had my breakfast there early one morning, cafe con leche and a croissant mind you but that was my breakfast. We ate at the ranchon to the side of the patio before the Cabaret Parisien show and don't remember finding it any good. I have yet to eat in the main dining room but have had their breakfast buffet at "La Veranda" on the lower floor and found it to be

pretty good. The Cabaret Parisien (restored in 2000) is a smaller version of the Tropicana show for a fraction of the price...and it's in the city close to everything. I remember being able to smoke my cigar while watching the show, I wonder if that's still allowed, you can't smoke at the Tropicana. I visited the pool on several occasions when I rented nearby. I loved it, no riff raff, mostly guests or mature people. There's a charge to use the pool if you're not a guest but most of that money can go towards buying food or drink poolside. They offer some great sandwiches and beer as well as a full bar with all the typical cocktails. For a few extra dollars I use the gym that's right next to the pool in an air-conditioned room, it has the basic stuff for a decent work out. The so-called "Buena Vista Social Club" play here in the salon Tuesday and Saturday nights but they aren't the guys we remember from the movie. Most of those people are dead and the band was never really a band except while touring for the movie. The random original member will turn up on occasion...the bass or trombone player, most of the main guys have passed away. One place that took me a long time to discover is what some people call the museum. It's a bar really, they call it the "hall of fame." An antique jukebox adorns the room as do many photos of celebrities that have visited the hotel. Of course there's a well-stocked bar in the room, excellent space for those evenings when the breeze coming off the ocean is a little too cool...it happens. One thing we can't forget is the cigar shop below the gift shop. The lovely and talented Milagro is the roller there. There's always a doorman waiting to open the entrance door for you and taxis are always sitting just outside to your left when exiting...if not, walk just outside the property.

As far as the hotel goes, although it's been showered with accolades through the years, I've heard from different people that have stayed there that except for the history and of course the patio, it's not one of the greatest hotels in the city, especially for what you're paying. For sure it's not the five stars it claims to be. The rooms are very outdated, some of them smelling of mold and because of the old plumbing sometimes there are issues in that department. The service is always talked about in a positive light and the issues (if any) are attended to. If a possible little inconvenience doesn't bother you, this is a wonderful hotel set in an excellent location with great restaurants and nightclubs within walking distance. You can't beat that patio, an excellent spot to end your evenings, and you never know who will show up.

Have you ever wondered why those cannons are on the back patio? Centuries ago, Havana was constantly attacked by pirates and after the English captured the city

in 1762 (being returned to Spain a year later) they decided to do something about it by building numerous fortifications including this one (now occupied by the hotel gardens) called the Santa Clara battery, which dates back to 1797. It was listed as a UNESCO World Heritage Site in 1982. The two cannons, the Krupp and the Ordóñez (the world's largest at the time) are what's left of the defense system that was installed here.

Guided tours of the hotel with an outline of its history are offered Monday to Friday at 10:00 a.m. and 4:00 p.m. as well as Saturday at 10:00 a.m. The hotel, with its 457 rooms, is 20 kilometers from the airport and 20 kilometers from playa Santa Maria (the beach). As well as the pool and gym that I mentioned earlier it also has tennis courts, sauna, and massage and medical services. Old Havana is a short taxi ride away but you don't need to go far for some great eateries and terrific nightlife.

After having mentioned the good and the bad you might ask, What am I saying? Should I book here or not? I have to say that for historical value, no other hotel tops this one but are the sentimental attributes worth more to you than modernity and convenience? That's a decision that only you can make and judge, so you will have to spend a holiday here to find out. If you're at all questioning it, I recommend you book it and partake in all of the hotel's many splendors when you do. I, myself, have never stayed in any of the rooms.

Here is a bit of history of the hotel: the Hotel Nacional de Cuba opened it's doors on the night of December 30, 1930 after fourteen months of construction. The who's who of guests that visited during this decade and the next are too many to mention: Johnny Weismuller (Tarzan) used to jump from a second story balcony into the pool; actor César Romero who was the grandchild of José Marti, as well as fellow actors George Raft, Frank Sinatra, Ava Gardner, Marlon Brando, John Wayne, Tyrone Power, Rita Hayworth, Buster Keaton, Fred Astaire, and Gary Cooper, just to name a few, and countless luminaries from the entertainment world and royalty.

Sir Winston Churchill was a guest here in 1946. There was a scene in the *Godfather II* where a meeting with all the capos takes place in a hotel in Havana. Although it didn't happen in the timeline shown in the movie, if Fidel Castro is entering the city victorious it meant it was 1959, it did actually take place in December 1946. The hotel closed its doors to the public while catering to the likes of Lucky Luciano, Meyer Lansky, Santo Trafficante Jr., Frank Costello, Albert Anastasia, and Vito Genovese as well as many others. By 1955, Lansky had a piece of the hotel and in 1957 the casino was making as much as any in Vegas. Although Nat King Cole at first was not allowed to stay in the hotel on racist grounds, it would be allowed after the memorable concerts he put on in the hotel. Eartha Kitt inaugurated the Cabaret Parisien in 1956.

On the triumph of the Revolution on January 1, 1959, the representatives of the American company that operated the hotel left and the hotel staff took over the management. Between 1960 and 1961, Cuba's revolutionary government reorganized the hotel's administration. The casino was closed in October 1960. Since there were no tourists during this time, the hotel was used to accommodate visiting diplomats and foreign government officials. With the collapse of the USSR, Cuba was forced to open its borders to tourism once again in the 1990s and after some restoration the hotel opened its doors to the world again in 1992. In 1998, the hotel was declared a national monument by the National Monuments Commission.

— M.S.

Hotel Nacional de Cuba
Calle 21 y O, Vedado, Havana, Cuba
Switchboard (53-7) 836 3564 & 67
E-Mail: reserva@hotelnacionaldecuba.com
Reservations Tel: (53-7) 838 0294 / 836 3564 ext. 598

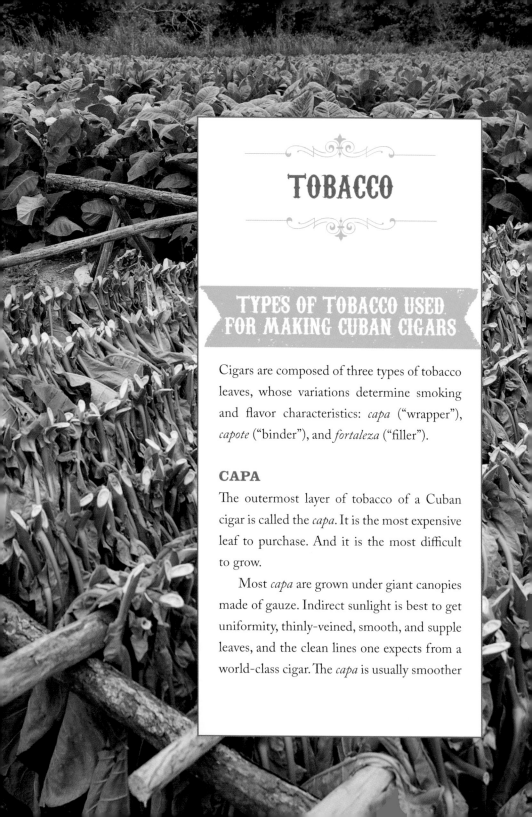

# TOBACCO

## TYPES OF TOBACCO USED FOR MAKING CUBAN CIGARS

Cigars are composed of three types of tobacco leaves, whose variations determine smoking and flavor characteristics: *capa* ("wrapper"), *capote* ("binder"), and *fortaleza* ("filler").

### CAPA

The outermost layer of tobacco of a Cuban cigar is called the *capa*. It is the most expensive leaf to purchase. And it is the most difficult to grow.

Most *capa* are grown under giant canopies made of gauze. Indirect sunlight is best to get uniformity, thinly-veined, smooth, and supple leaves, and the clean lines one expects from a world-class cigar. The *capa* is usually smoother in taste to the smoker. More often than not, the wrappers are fermented separately from the binder and filler. In general, dark wrappers add a touch of sweetness, while light ones add a hint of dryness to the taste.

More than anything else, it is the *capa* that gives a cigar its character and flavor. And the color of those leaves are often used to describe the cigar as a whole.

**Candela (Double Claro):** Very light, slightly greenish. These leaves are picked before they fully ripen, retaining some of the chlorophyll that gives them their distinctive green coloration. They are dried quickly to help retain that color.

**Claro:** Very light tan or yellowish.

**Colorado Claro:** Medium brown.

**Colorado (Rosado):** Reddish-brown.

**Colorado Maduro:** Darker brown.

**Maduro:** Very dark brown.

**Oscuro (Double Maduro):** Black.

Double Claro · Claro · Colorado Claro · Colorado · Colorado Maduro · Maduro · Oscuro

## CAPOTE

Beneath the wrapper is a small wadding of tobacco leaves that's referred to in English as "binder." These are the tobaccos just under the *capa*, or wrapper. *Capote* is made from the upper most leaves of the tobacco plant, the ones that get the most sun. They are chosen because they are pliable and durable for rolling. While the *capa* must be shade grown, unblemished, and smooth, *capote* leaves can exhibit discoloration or blemishes. More often than not, *capote* leaves are much thicker and have more heft than *capa*.

## FORTALEZA

*Fortaleza* is the bunched up tobacco in the middle of the cigar and it can be made of "long filler" or "short filler." *Fortaleza* comes in three degrees: *volado* ("mild"), *seco* ("medium-bodied") and *ligero* ("strong" or "bold").

While some aficionados prefer long filler, hand-rolled cigars, other experts argue that ones made with short filler offer the producer the

### ★ TOO TIGHT. TOO LOOSE. ★

As the cigar is made, how tightly the filler (made of blended leaves from varying parts of the tobacco plant) is packed significantly impacts the final smoke. Some air passages need to be created so that air can flow through the length of the cigar. If the filler is too tightly packed, it will be exceedingly difficult for the smoker to draw air through the length of the cigar and therefore be near impossible to smoke. A cigar with too much air (packed too loosely) will burn too quickly and will not provide that enjoyable drawn out smoking experience.

opportunity to shape the flavor of the cigar.

By using different parts of the plant, the manufacturer can control or manipulate the flavor profile of the cigar. For example, *volado* is taken from the bottom leaves of the plant and offers a mild taste and burns more easily. *Seco* is made from the middle leaves of the plant, and offers a somewhat more medium-bodied flavor profile. *Ligero* comes from the sun-drenched, top part of the plant. It's the slowest burning of the fillers and is generally packed into the middle of the filler. It also offers the strongest flavor.

## ★ LONG FILLER VS. ★ SHORT FILLER

If full leaves are used as filler, a cigar is said to be composed of "long filler." There is a consistency in the relative slow burn of a long filler that helps bring the built up flavors through in the cigar. Cigars made from smaller bits of leaf, or chopped tobacco, including many machine-made cigars, are said to be made of "short filler." These tend to burn hotter and faster than long filler cigars, and some critics contend that they lack the complexity of long filler cigars.

# ★ A VISIT WITH HECTOR LUIS PRIETO ★ AT HIS TOBACCO PLANTATION IN THE PROVINCE OF PINAR DEL RIO, CUBA

I met Hector a few years ago on his farm the year after he had won the Hombre Habano award, one of Cuba's highest cigar honors, in 2009. When he won the award previously in 2008, he was the youngest man to have ever done so. Almost five years have gone by and some very notable changes have taken place on his property. What was once a dream of his has now become a reality. A lovely Ranchon with a stocked bar (and electricity to power my laptop) has been built, which can accommodate a good number of people. He's all set up to receive large groups of tourists who take tours along the Tobacco Route in the Pinar del Rio region of Cuba. He finally finished building his house and also had a nice humidor/ office erected where he keeps his Habano award as well as his personal stock of cigars—he's an avid smoker. I found Hector more laid back than I did the last time, he seems to have settled in nicely to his new-found fame. I also found tobacco growing when it shouldn't have been. The previous year's growing season, which is usually between November and February, was horrible. Most everyone lost a good deal of their crops due to way too much rain. However, the spring has proven to be ideal for growing tobacco this year so why not take advantage of the great conditions and make up for lost product. I was assured the quality of the leaf would be no different and the quality of tobacco on this plantation is one of the best in Cuba.

Miquel, the ever animated house roller, is still there and still rolling some of the best cigars on this side of the island. I met him before he worked for Hector while he rolled cigars for another farmer. You can't pay a visit to one of these places and not have one of their house specialties...I had two. Everything seems to be fine as I found everyone relaxed and in good spirits.

— M.S.

Cuba is one of the best tobacco growing regions in the world. But just because it's grown in Cuba doesn't mean it ends up in a Cuban cigar. Only the best leaves are chosen to be in the world's best cigars.

Just like in the world of wine, tobacco aficionados believe in terroir—a specific character of color, texture, and flavor that are intimately connected with the land where the tobacco is grown. Each growing region is strictly limited to certified defined areas, zones, and districts of Cuba and are awarded a special status as Protected Denomination of Origin (D.O.P.). Even within those regions, only a certain small number of plantations grow acceptable tobacco.

Some plantations are awarded the distinction *Vegas Finas de Primera* ("first class fields"), which are rated higher than all others for their exceptional soil quality and microclimate. Also, the skill of the growers in these regions is unmatched by any other.

## PINAR DEL RÍO

Pinar del Río is the western province of Cuba that is home to some of the most important tobacco growing regions of Cuba and known for its unusual landscape of limestone mountains (*mogotes*). It's

also the name of the D.O.P. inside of which there are several tobacco zones: Vuelta Abajo, Semi Vuelta, and districts including San Juan y Martínez and San Luis.

## Vuelta Abajo

Critics and connoisseurs agree, Vuelta Abajo is the best cigar tobacco-growing region in the world. A product of the distinctive rich red soil of the Vuelta Abajo, the tobacco grown in this region is hands down the best tobacco, both for filler and wrapper. The region serves as the main source of tobacco for the best cigars of Cuba, and the only zone that grows all types of leaf: wrappers, filler, and binders. Many critics contend that the secret to the quality of the tobacco from this region relies on the fact that the leaves contain a high concentration of nitrate, which provides an ample amount of flavor and structure seldom seen, to this degree, in tobacco grown in other regions. The singular climate in this region yields such unique characteristics and beloved cigars.

## San Luis

San Luis is the small town in the Pinar Del Río province at the epi-

TOBACCO REGIONS
- PINAR DEL RIO*
- PARTIDO*
- REMEDIOS*
- VUELTA ARRIBA*

center of Cuban tobacco culture. The town is known for the cultivation of wrapper leaves. As a district in the Vuelta Abajo zone it's protected as a D.O.P. World-famous farms such as El Corojo Vega and Cuchillas de Barbacoa are found here. Leaves supplied for the Cohiba brand are grown in this district, one of two that are known for having the best *vegas*.

## San Juan y Martínez

The other small but celebrated town in Vuelta Abajo that is protected as a D.O.P. is San Juan y Martínez. The town holds a reputation for the cultivation of fillers and binders and is home to the famous Hoyo de Monterrey plantation. Like San Luis, San Juan y Martínez's finest *vegas* also grow and supply leaves for Cohiba cigars.

## Semi Vuelta

The Semi Vuelta region is mainly known for its cultivation of binder and thicker filler leaves. It's east of the Vuelta Abajo but still within the Pinar del Río border, providing strong soil for seeds. These seeds will eventually return to the Vuelta Abajo region. Most Semi Vuelta tobacco is grown for use in the national cigarettes, since it is not desirable enough for cigar quality.

## PARTIDO

Partido is a historic tobacco region, established in the 17th century and situated in the southwest region of Havana City. Partido is mainly known for the cultivation of wrapper leaves and is protected as a D.O.P.

## VUELTA ARRIBA

Vuelta Arriba is the name of the two large growing regions, including the Remedios tobacco-growing areas in the central and eastern part of Cuba. This region supplies filler and binder for some of Cuba's best cigars.

## REMEDIOS

Remedios, founded in 1578 by Spain and known as the oldest tobacco-growing region of Cuba, is a protected D.O.P. Located in the center of Cuba, and also host to many sugar plantations, the soil and climate of Remedios is characteristically rich and fertile. The pre-revolution José L. Piedra cigars, established in the 1880s, are produced in this region.

## ORIENTE

Oriente is at the extreme eastern end of Cuba. In 1492, Columbus landed in Bariay, in that region, and discovered Cuban tobacco. Like other tobacco growing regions in the area, it is protected as a D.O.P.

Tobacco, like wine, benefits from aging. Tobacco may be stored before manufacture or cigars may be aged after being rolled. Age will benefit both. Both processes have their fans and their detractors.

### AGING TOBACCO LEAVES

Once tobacco is harvested, it's customarily hung and air-dried for approximately thirty days. This is referred to as curing. When it's picked at its fullest maturity the leaves are green, and during this curing process the leaves will change over the course of thirty days from green to yellow to reddish-orange to brown.

*Capa* leaves, or wrapper leaves, are usually cured in large barns or sheds. These buildings are fully enclosed to keep moisture and weather off these leaves and,

depending on the season, the leaves are often heated with charcoal, gas, wood, or propane to help the curing process along. *Capote* and *fortaleza*, binder and filler, are usually stored in open sheds to provide maximum airflow. These buildings may have slats throughout or just large, opened doors to maximize airflow and drying of the leaves.

*Capote* and *fortaleza* are aged in large bales called *pacas*. These *pacas* can weigh approximately 4,000 to 5,000 pounds, or two to two-and-a-half tons. The *pacas* are wrapped in burlap and shaped like giant bales of hay or cubes. The mois-

ture and breakdown of the plant matter create heat. The *pacas* are monitored, and weekly, opened up, turned over, and reconstituted. The material inside is rotated to ensure

even processing throughout the bundle.

Depending on the particular type of tobacco, *volado* ("mild"), *seco* ("medium-bodied") and *ligero* ("strong" or "bold") are stored for up to six months.

*Capa* leaves are aged in *tericos*. These are bundles or bales of wrapper leaves wrapped in large pieces of *yagua*. *Yagua* is the loose part of the bark of the Royal Palm, Cuba's national tree.

# ALL ABOUT CIGARS

### VITOLA

*Vitola* refers to the size and shape of a cigar. In Spain, it is the term for the cigar band or ring. Below are charts of the varying cigar sizes within the industry. The two dominant groups of cigar sizes are *Parejos* and *Figurados*.

### Parejo

*Parejo* is the most common cigar shape and it refers to cigars with straight sides. Almost all the cigars in this category take on the relative shape of a *Corona*. These cigars have a cylindrical body, straight sides, one end open, and a round tobacco-leaf "cap" on the other end. This rounded tip is the one that gets either pierced or cut by the consumer before smoking.

Here is a list of the different type of *Parejos*:

| VITOLA | LENGTH | RING | GAUGE |
|---|---|---|---|
| Gran Corona | 9 | ¼ | 47 |
| Prominentes | 7 | ⅝ | 49 |
| Laguito Especial (pigtail) | 7 | ½ | 40 |
| Laguito No. 1 (pigtail) | 7 | ½ | 38 |
| Delicados | 7 | ½ | 38 |
| Delicados Extra | 7 | ½ | 36 |
| Paco | 7 | ⅛ | 49 |
| Julieta No. 2 | 7 | | 47 |
| Ninfas | 7 | | 33 |
| Panetelas Largas | 6 | ⅞ | 28 |
| Dalias | 6 | ¾ | 43 |
| Palmas | 6 | ¾ | 33 |
| Hermosos No.1 | 6 | ⅝ | 48 |
| Cervantes | 6 | ½ | 42 |
| Parejos | 6 | ½ | 38 |
| Cazadores | 6 | ⅜ | 43 |
| Deliciosos | 6 | ¼ | 33 |
| Dobles (pigtail) | 6 | ⅛ | 50 |
| Coronas Grandes | 6 | ⅛ | 42 |
| Cazadores JLP | 6 | | 43 |
| Laguito No. 2 | 6 | | 38 |
| Palmitas | 6 | | 32 |
| Canonazo | 5 | ¾ | 52 |
| Exquisitos | 5 | ¾ | 46 |
| Conservas | 5 | ¾ | 43 |
| Cristales | 5 | ¾ | 41 |
| Corona Gordas | 5 | ⅝ | 46 |

| VITOLA | LENGTH | RING | GAUGE |
| --- | --- | --- | --- |
| Franciscos | 5 | ⅝ | 44 |
| Coronas | 5 | ⅝ | 42 |
| Carlotas | 5 | ⅝ | 35 |
| Genios | 5 | ½ | 52 |
| Conservas JLP | 5 | ½ | 44 |
| Nacionales | 5 | ½ | 41 |
| Cremas | 5 | ½ | 40 |
| Edmundo | 5 | ⅜ | 52 |
| Dalias Cortas | 5 | ⅜ | 43 |
| Cosacos | 5 | ⅜ | 42 |
| Cremas JLP | 5 | ⅜ | 40 |
| Coloniales (pigtail) | 5 | ¼ | 44 |
| Nacionales JLP (134mm) | 5 | ¼ | 42 |
| Brevas JLP (133mm) | 5 | ¼ | 42 |
| Eminentes (132mm) | 5 | ¼ | 42 |
| Gordito | 5 | ⅕ | 50 |
| Marevas | 5 | ⅛ | 42 |
| Petit Coronas | 5 | ⅛ | 42 |
| Almuerzos (139mm) | 5 | ⅛ | 40 |
| Petit Cetros (138mm) | 5 | ⅛ | 40 |
| Hermosos No. 4 | 5 | | 48 |
| Londres | 5 | | 40 |
| Belvedere | 5 | | 39 |
| Petit Cetros JLP | 5 | | 38 |
| Vegueritos | 5 | | 36 |
| Conchitas | 5 | | 35 |
| Placeras | 5 | | 34 |
| Seoane | 5 | | 33 |
| Standard | 4 | ⅞ | 40 |
| Petit Edmundo | 4 | ¾ | 52 |
| Carolinas | 4 | ¾ | 29 |

| VITOLA | LENGTH | RING | GAUGE |
| --- | --- | --- | --- |
| Robustos (117mm) | 4 | ⅝ | 50 |
| Coronitas (116mm) | 4 | ⅝ | 40 |
| Franciscanos | 4 | ⅝ | 40 |
| Sports | 4 | ⅝ | 35 |
| Magicos | 4 | ½ | 52 |
| Cadetes | 4 | ½ | 36 |
| Laguito No. 3 | 4 | ½ | 26 |
| Minutos | 4 | ⅜ | 42 |
| Reyes (pigtail) | 4 | ⅜ | 40 |
| Secretos | 4 | ⅜ | 40 |
| Trabucos | 4 | ⅜ | 38 |
| Epicures | 4 | ⅜ | 35 |
| Petit Cazadores | 4 | ⅛ | 43 |
| Petit Robustos | 4 | | 50 |
| Perlas | 4 | | 40 |
| Entreactos | 4 | | 30 |

The above figures and dimensions may vary slightly depending on producer and the roller.

## Figurado

While *Parejos* are the more traditional and common shapes, there are many popular cigars that fall under the heading *Figurados*. These are irregularly shaped cigars. Some are considered of higher quality, simply because they are so hard to make and they require greater skill by the rollers.

*Figurados* dominated the nineteenth century in terms of popularity. By the 1930s, the more traditional *Corona* shape overtook the market but in the last few decades these shapes and styles have made a resounding comeback.

*Figurados* include the following:

| VITOLA | LENGTH | RING | GAUGE | TYPE |
| --- | --- | --- | --- | --- |
| Diadema | 8 | ⅞ | 55 | diadema |
| Salomon | 7 | ¼ | 57 | diadema |
| Rodolfo | 7 | ⅛ | 54 | pyramid |
| Romeo | 6 | ⅜ | 52 | perfecto |
| Tacos | 6 | ¼ | 47 | diadema |
| Piramides | 6 | ⅛ | 52 | pyramid |
| Culebras | 5 | ¾ | 39 | culebra |
| Campanas | 5 | ½ | 52 | torpedo |
| Generosos | 5 | ¼ | 42 | diadema |
| Favoritos | 4 | ¾ | 42 | diadema |
| Petit Bouquet | 4 | | 43 | perfecto |

## CIGARILLO

A cigarillo is an "in-betweener." A cigarillo is a machine-made cigar that tends to be narrower and shorter than a traditional cigar. However, it is also larger than a little cigar. Cigarillos are usually not filtered, but may exhibit plastic or wood filter tips. These should not be misinterpreted: They are not meant to be inhaled.

## LITTLE CIGARS

Little cigars, also called small cigars or miniatures, in many ways, differ from regular cigars. They weigh less than cigars and cigarillos, and they particularly resemble cigarettes in filters, packaging, shape, and size.

These cigars have an overall feel and draw similiar to cigarettes, but use fermented and aged tobaccos. Filtered cigars are supposedly close to traditional cigars, and are not meant to be inhaled.

# ★ PROFILES OF CIGAR ROLLERS OF CUBA ★

## JUANITA, THE HOUSE ROLLER AT HOTEL MELIA COHIBA

No trip to Havana would be complete without visiting the lovely Juanita who rolls some spectacular cigars at the Hotel Meliá Cohiba.

As always, I found her in good spirits and thanks to the powers that be, in good health as well. I enjoyed standing beside her table and watching her roll as we chat about what's going on in the world of cigars and Cuba. We could talk for hours, but I try to limit my time here because of other previous commitments.

I noticed a lot more Americans approaching her table on this trip. Consider this an update to let all her fans know that, as of this writing, she's okay and still rolling some of the best cigars in Havana.

This lady has won the hearts of many cigar aficionados from around the world; I know a few of them. She is an absolutely delightful human being that has such a positive aura about her that it's difficult to leave her side. I myself have not had the good fortune of knowing her a long time. I met her several years ago, but didn't really get to know her until this interview. I've had friends rave about how spectacular her cigars are. After having smoked a few, they do deserve to be classified up there in the higher echelons of cigar classification but then it all becomes personal taste. What does that mean? She rolls a really good cigar.

Juanita was born in Havana on January 27, 1956. She was studying to become a teacher when just one year before graduation her father told her to drop out and become a roller. At that time, there was a big push to have women rollers, before the Revolution only men were rolling cigars. In 1973, she graduated from roller's school and began working at El Laguito (the Cohiba factory), a project that had been initiated by Celia Sanchez, Fidel Castro's right hand. Eventually, Juanita even taught young rollers at El Laguito.

I found that very interesting, especially since I recently read a book about Celia Sanchez and knew a little about some of the projects she was involved in, El Laguito included.

Juanita is single at this time and has two children, both boys, ages 30 and 39. Her mother is still alive but her father died recently, he was hit by a car at age 101. I've always seen her in a good mood and anyone I've seen interact with her has always seemed to sincerely enjoy her presence. I have now joined those ranks.

Q. How many cigars do you roll per day?
A. Thirty to thirty-five per day, sometimes more.

Q. Have you traveled anywhere outside the country?
A. For reasons of work I've been to Switzerland, Germany, Austria, Italy,
and I lived in Russia for five years when my husband at the time was in the
military.

Q. Do you have a favorite vitola you like to roll?
A. I specialize in Robustos and Lanceros. I learned to roll the Lancero at El
Laguito.

Q. Who do you see buying more of your cigars, from what country?
A. The Germans, Chinese, Italians, Canadians, and Arabs buy more.

Q. Are you a sports fan?
A. I like gymnastics but recently I've begun watching baseball.

Q. Who is the most famous person that you know of that has smoked one
of your cigars?
A. The Prince of Qatar, Cesar Lopez (famous jazz musician) and Fidel
Castro...whose cigar kept going out because he talks so much.
(He later assured her the cigar was excellent and that she did a great job.)

Q. Name three people you would love to smoke a cigar with, dead or alive.
A. My son who is in the United States, Alejandro Robaina, and Fidel Castro.

Q. How do you get your tobacco and who chooses the blend?
A. The head office sends me the tobacco and I decide the blend.

   If you're ever in the neighborhood, drop in and say hello to Juanita and
pick up one of her cigars and give it a try. You can be sure that it will be one
of the better rolled cigars you'll ever hold.

## ALEJANDRO GONZALEZ ARIAS,
## THE HOUSE ROLLER AT HOTEL COMODORO HAVANA

The chair behind the roller's bench had been empty for several months at the Hotel Comodoro Cigar Shop in the Miramar district of Havana. Anyone who knew the previous roller, Crisantos, was anxiously awaiting who would fill that seat. For those of you who don't know, Crisantos was known to be one of the best rollers in the city. He vacated his position due to retirement. I for one had made several visits to the shop while it had no roller. Knowing everyone there (excellent service) and being close to where I stay when I'm in Havana, having no roller didn't stop me from dropping in. I enjoy smoking a cigar and having a chat with the store manager Andre who has become a friend over the years. On my trip in January the replacement had finally arrived. I had the pleasure of meeting him the week he started but didn't have the time to have a lengthy chat. However, this trip I prepared to have a sit down and ask him a few questions.

Alex is very young to be in this position, the youngest roller I know working in a cigar shop. Most of the rollers in the cigar shops in Cuba, male or female, are all around retirement age or nearing it. That doesn't mean he can't roll a cigar. As a matter of fact he does a fantastic job. I have yet to try all his vitolas but I can tell you his signature Behike 52 is the bomb. Watch out for this guy, he's only 28 and I can't imagine what he's going to be like twenty to thirty years from now. Born in July 1986, single with no children, he's never traveled outside the country and lives almost within walking distance of the hotel.

**1. How long have you been in the industry and do you have any family members that are in it?**
I've been rolling for six to seven years and have no family members in the industry.

**2. How did you know you wanted to do this and what was the process?**

I was working at the market at the Marina Hemingway and there was a roller there. Everyday I would watch the roller and in time we became friends. She could tell I was interested and one day asked me if I wanted to learn how to roll cigars. She taught me the basics but I took the course at the El Laguito factory to become a roller.

**3. What is your favorite vitola to roll?**

The Behike 52.

**4. How many cigars do you smoke a day and what do you like to drink with them?**

I smoke one cigar a day, I like to test what I'm rolling, it's my way of doing a quality check. When the moment allows me I like to drink a whiskey with my cigar.

**5. Were you nervous knowing you would be taking over Crisantos' old position?**

No, I knew what I was getting into and the prestige that this cigar shop's roller's table held. Customers are surprised to see me there and not Crisantos but little by little I'm winning them over. It's a long process but I do the best I can and hopefully I will be accepted.

### 6. How many cigars do you roll a day and who picks the leaf?

The amount of cigars I roll a day depends on demand. Right now it's about ten to twenty per day. The leaf is sent to us by Habanos but I have the right to inspect it before accepting it and if it doesn't meet my standards I can send it back.

### 7. What's your favorite sport?

Squash. (The answer actually surprised me...do they even have squash courts here?)

### 8. Really?? I meant to watch?

Football. (Which means soccer to us North Americans)

### 9. What about baseball and do you have a favorite team?

What Cuban doesn't like baseball. Industriales is my favorite baseball team. When it comes to soccer, I like it all as long as it's a good game but if I had to pick a team, Barcelona.

Alex is a very personable young man who doesn't seem to have an ego. I bumped into a couple of Canadians visiting the shop while Alex was out and asked them what they thought of his cigars. They answered that they loved Crisantos' but that Alex's are better. When I told Alex about the encounter and what he thought about what they said he answered with embarrassment: "No, they're not better, just different, every roller has his *liga* (blend) and every smoker has a preference. Mine are not better, they may just appeal to some more than others." I can tell you that his signature cigar, the Behike 52, is fantastic and is worth the visit to shop to try (and buy). As for his other Vitolas, I purchased one of each and will try them in the near future. While I was there I was looking for something long and skinny, like a Lancero, but he didn't have any. He had me pick the Vitola I wanted from a book and within the hour I had my cigars...I loved it. Watch out for this guy and pay him a visit.

Alejandro (Alex) Gonzalez Arias

Hotel Comodoro

3ra y Calle 84

Miramar, Playa, Havana

tel. 204-5551 ext.1272

— M.S.

The word habanos simply means something originating from Havana. So it is only appropriate that the national Cuban state tobacco company, Cubatabaco (a sort of acronym for "Empresa Cubana del Tabaco") established Habanos S.A. (Sociedad Anomina) in 1994 as the governmental department that monitors the production and distribution of Cuban tobacco around the world. In addition, Habanos S.A. owns all the Cuban cigar brands and Cuban cigarettes sold and distributed worldwide. Habanos S.A. has identified the following special production cigars that have been approved by the Regulatory Council for the Protected Denomination of Origin (D.O.P.).

## RESERVA

The term "Reserva" describes the Habanos cigars where all of the leaves—fillers, binders, and wrappers—were aged in bales for a minimum of three years before being transported to the factory to be rolled.

Special leaves from the Vuelta Abajo region are used to make Reserva Habanos.

Using tobaccos from the 1999 harvest, the Cohiba Seleccion Reserva was released in 2003, the first of this type of specialty. Likewise, the Partagás Serie D No. 4 Reserva used leaves grown in 2000 and the Montecristo No. 4 Reserva from tobaccos harvested in 2002.

Traditionally for each release of Reserva Habanos, only a limited number are made. They are packaged in 5,000 exclusive boxes of twenty Habanos. Each box is elegant and individually numbered by Habanos S.A. Each cigar boasts the second band of black and silver, marked it as a Reserva.

## GRAN RESERVA

The term "Gran Reserva" is for only the Habanos whose leaves (fillers, binders, and wrappers) have aged for a minimum of five years before going to the factory for rolling.

The finest leaves from the Vuelta Abajo region are picked to withstand this particular aging process, so that they will deliver the flavor and aroma expected of these Habanos.

The first of this particular Habanos used tobaccos from 2003, and was released in 2009. Selecting the Cohiba Siglo VI size, fifteen cigars were contained within only 5,000 elegant boxes, each Habano numbered and identified with a black and gold Gran Reserva band.

Following this, a second Gran Reserva size was released in 2011—the Montecristo No. 2, which used tobaccos from 2005.

## EDICIÓN LIMITADA

The first Edición Limitada (Limited Edition Habanos) were released in 2000 for the first time. Limited Edition wrappers are referred to as Oscuro, which come from higher points on a shade-grown plant. These leaves tend to be thicker and darker than the usual wrapper on a Habanos.

Because these leaves are thicker, they need more time to ferment and age, which is about two or so years in bales before the Habanos are rolled.

When first introduced in 2000, it was only the Oscuro wrappers on Limited Editions that were made with specially extra-aged leaves. But after 2007, fillers and binders were also aged for at least two years for this type of cigar.

The boxes carry an extra black and gold seal indicating that they contain Limited Edition cigars and give the year when they were released.

## COHIBA MADURO 5

There are two distinct ways the Cohiba Maduro 5 differs from other cigars in this section: First, because the Cohiba Maduro 5 is a standard line—not a specialty Habano—or second, because only one of its leaves uses an extra-aged tobacco leaf, the dark maduro wrapper. This cigar serves as an example of this particular combination.

Introduced in 2007, all three sizes (Genios, 5½ inches by 52 ring; Mágicos, 4½ inches by 52 ring; and Secretos, 4⅓ inches by 40) in Cohiba's Linea Maduro 5 are wrapped with these dark maduro leaves for uniformity. Cohiba's Linea Maduro 5 uses the wrappers harvested from the top-most levels of shade-grown plants, which must be dark and aged enough to be called "maduro."

The maduro leaves, which are naturally dried to optimum age and color, demand extra fermentation and ageing. In this case, they are left in bales to mature for about five years before being added to the cigars, hence the number "5" in the line's name.

In the world of Habanos, opinions may differ over the wrapper's influence on taste, but few would argue that Cuban maduro wrappers bring certain sweetness and full-body aroma to the flavor.

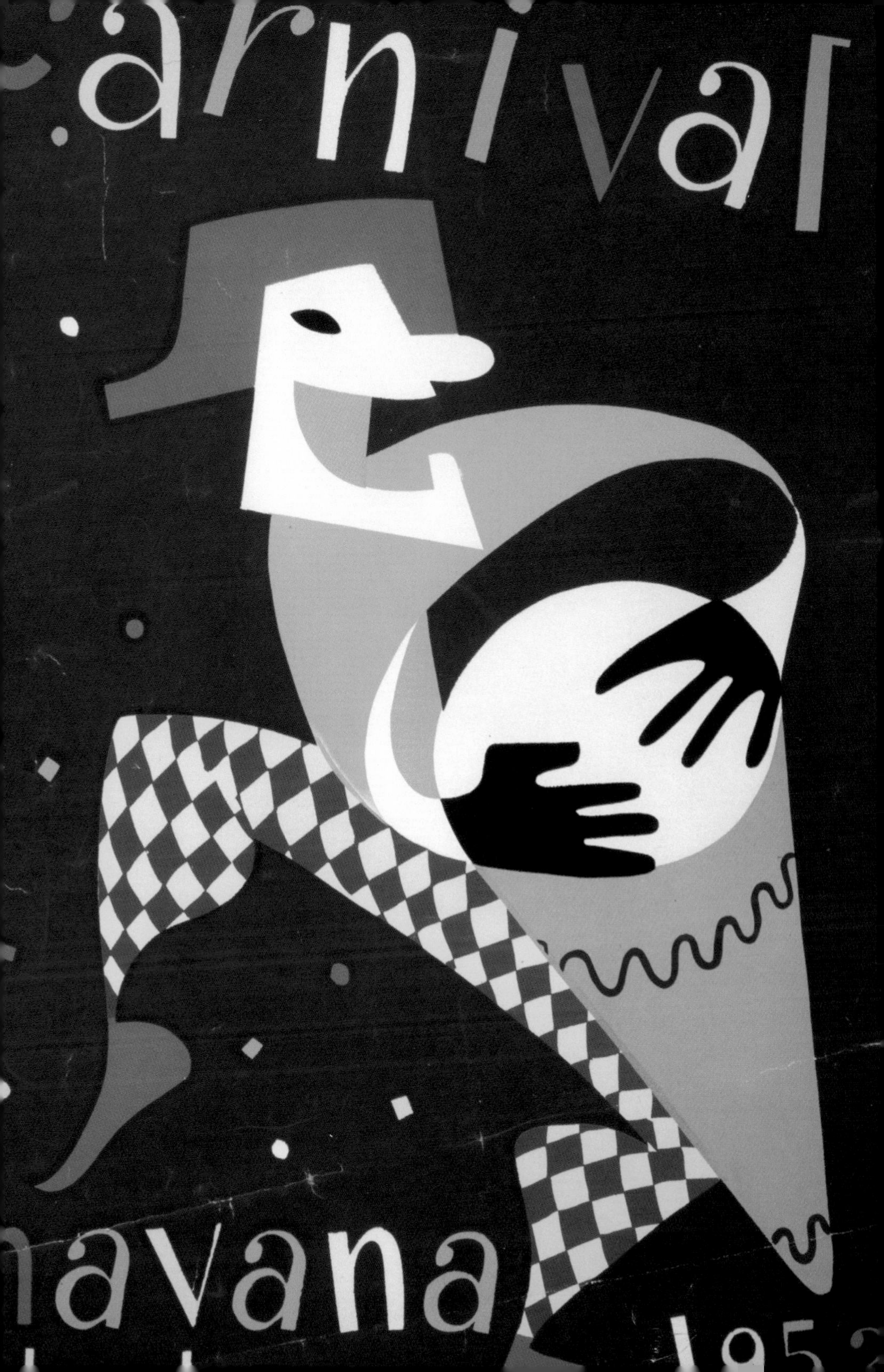
carnival
avana
195

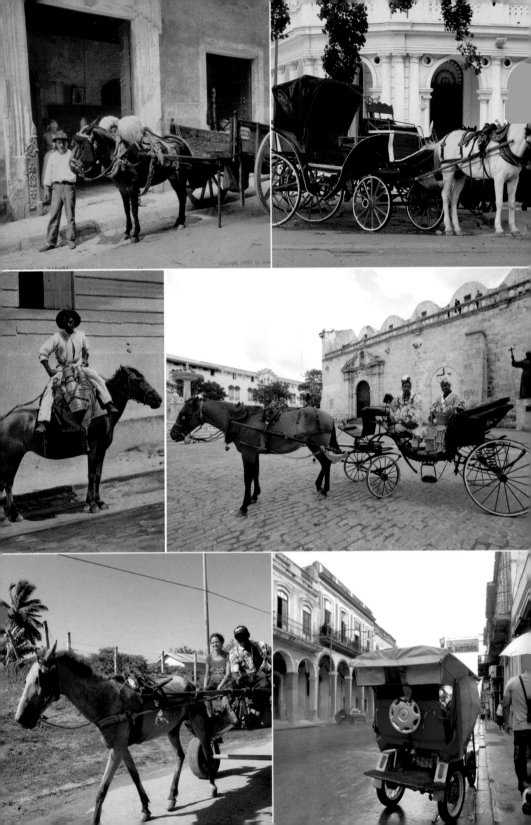

# ✭ CUBAN TRANSPORTATION ✭

When I say "Cuban transportation," I'm sure that images of classic American automobiles from the 50s come to mind. Even though there have been changes with relations between the U.S. and Cuban governments, that means of transportation is still the most evident, or the one that tourists remember the most.  However, this post isn't about that kind of transportation, it's about everything else.

The collapse of the Soviet Union had a tremendous effect on the Cuban economy; especially in its capacity to buy oil, which they got cheap from the Soviets before they pulled out. That cheap oil ended in 1990 and the so-called "Special Period," as Fidel Castro dubbed it, had begun. Sacrifices had to be made and alternate means of transportation had to be found (or used). In 1995 Cuba was functioning on half the energy it was in 1991. The bicycle was one of those means of transportation that was embraced during this period. There was virtually no cyclist culture before 1990. The bike was once thought of as a recreation, it now was to be used as a necessity. People traded jobs in order to be close enough to bike to work. More than one million bicycles were bought from China and sold for a fraction of the cost to Cubans. An industry flourished within Cuba that began to manufacture 150,000 bikes per year. There is an estimated two million bikes in Cuba today, half a million are in Havana.

Another form of transportation that was born from the bicycle but not invented in Cuba was the BiciTaxi. It's basically a type of rickshaw that the government started licensing in the early 1990s (late compared to other countries with similar transportation) with the advent of self-employment due to the government's necessity. The garishly decorated three-wheeled bicycle taxis, some sporting massive sound systems, have often been criticized and slapped with unfair laws. The government even made a push with the CocoTaxi to try and drive them out but they are here to stay and part of the landscape not only here but in towns and cities scattered all over Cuba. They're a pain in the rear-end when you're driving a car and find one in front of you on a narrow road but it's just part of the experience of Cuba. They were only allowed to move Cubans at one time and I'm not sure if that law has changed but I've taken a ride on one a couple of times, one of them being in the pouring rain. When it rains they pull out a tarp, which covers the passengers, perfect for me on that ride. Always negotiate a price before you begin your ride. They take the Cuban National Peso, but of course they will take CUC as well. The CocoTaxi is a horrible tourist trap in my opinion, which you only find in the tourist areas of Havana. Originally priced in the Cuban National Peso, it now only takes CUC and lots of them. There is no fare list and it's very over-priced in comparison to other forms of transportation. It's called a CocoTaxi because they resemble a coconut. Basically, it's an Italian three-wheeled moped topped with a coconut shaped fiberglass body with no seat belts.

However, the transformation of the transportation was not limited to bicycles. The farther out you go from Havana, the more animals you will see on the roads. Of course these animals are mostly horses but not limited to a one man on one horse style. Outside of Havana you will find horses pulling more than just the usual array of carriages. It seems that Cuba has taken taxiing people around to a whole new level. Everything becomes a bus...even dump trucks.

Needless to say, Cuba has responded exceptionally well in the face of hard times in the form of a lack of fuel. It's very evident in the numerous forms or transformed means of mass transportation that you find along the highways and byways on the island. In the countryside it seems that the beast of burden and the horse rule the roads and in some parts they're the only means that can get you to your destination. It definitely adds to the color of the country and makes for some wonderful photography.

— M.S.

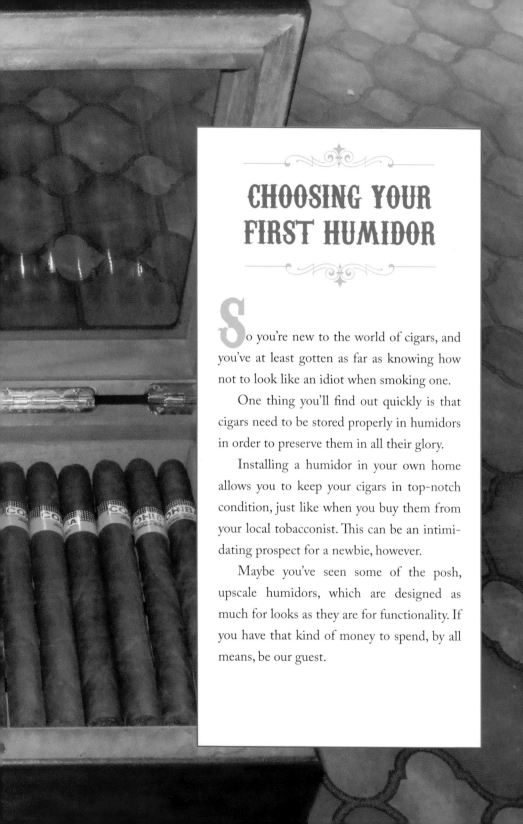

# CHOOSING YOUR FIRST HUMIDOR

**S**o you're new to the world of cigars, and you've at least gotten as far as knowing how not to look like an idiot when smoking one.

One thing you'll find out quickly is that cigars need to be stored properly in humidors in order to preserve them in all their glory.

Installing a humidor in your own home allows you to keep your cigars in top-notch condition, just like when you buy them from your local tobacconist. This can be an intimidating prospect for a newbie, however.

Maybe you've seen some of the posh, upscale humidors, which are designed as much for looks as they are for functionality. If you have that kind of money to spend, by all means, be our guest.

If you don't though, read on for advice about purchasing your first humidor without breaking the bank.

But first, let's take a look briefly at where humidors came from.

## HISTORY OF THE HUMIDOR

The concept of the humidor is usually traced backed to an Irish furniture craftsman named Terence Manning, who in the year 1887 returned home to Ireland after spending time abroad honing his skills. The Manning family created and distributed the earliest known humidors, and they are still in the business today.

Early humidors were made of fine wood and were quite expensive. Nowadays there are many less expensive versions of humidors made of cheaper materials which still get the job done—usually wood board, metal or acrylic glass with an internal layer of wood.

Gerry G. Schmidt in Newport Beach, California invented portable humidors in 1998. Collectible wood humidors remain popular among cigar smokers however, and can make a great addition to your household if you have the budget.

## CLASSIFICATIONS OF HUMIDORS

There are several different types of humidors, classified according to capacity and purpose. The type of humidor you should buy depends on your needs. We'll discuss size and capacity later on in the article.

**Room/walk-in humidors.** You would only need a room humidor if you were operating a shop, were a cigar supplier or distributor, or if you were a major collector. This is literally a room that has been converted into a humidor.

**Cabinet and table humidors.** These are high capacity humidors, which can hold thousands of cigars.

Cabinet humidors are pieces of furniture in their own right, while table humidors are more portable, but rarely moved since they likewise are generally huge and heavy. You probably do not need or want either of these types of humidors as a beginner, but you may want one later on.

**Personal and portable humidors.** These are both humidor types that may interest you. A personal humidor is the first humidor you will likely buy, and will allow you to hold a few dozen cigars. These containers are small, relatively lightweight, and movable. Portable humidors are miniature versions that allow you to carry up to around a dozen cigars. They're great when you're traveling.

In terms of design, there are all kinds of different aesthetic choices out there, ranging from the simplest rectangular boxes to ornate wood boxes with rounded edges and artistic flourishes. You also may find humidors with glass lids, which allow you to see inside. The design you choose is entirely up to your personal preferences.

As mentioned before, materials for modern humidors typically

include wood board, metal or acrylic glass. Other modern humidors are made entirely out of wood. Common choices for wood include mahogany, cherry, walnut, oak, maple, and pine.

Larger humidors like cabinet and table humidors may be made out of a heavier material like marble. Some may even have leather exteriors.

The ideal material for the interior of a humidor is usually considered to be Spanish cedar. This type of wood is beautiful, but the choice is also functional. It can withstand humidity that would cause other types of wood to warp and lose shape over time.

## DO YOU EVEN NEED A HUMIDOR?

First off, how many cigars do you actually have?

If you still don't have a big collection, you may not need a humidor yet, especially if you have some handy household supplies like zip lock bags.

At that rate, if you have a cooler, you can actually use that as a makeshift humidor. This is such a common solution that there's even a colloquial expression for a cooler-turned-humidor: a "coolidor." As your collection grows though, a real humidor is something you're going to want.

## HOW LARGE SHOULD IT BE?

Ask yourself how many boxes of cigars you think you'll have around at a given time. Consider that a box of cigars may hold up to 25 cigars. So multiply by that number to figure out how much space you're going to need.

Buying a humidor that is just slightly larger than what you think you'll need is usually a good plan since it gives you more flexibility without wasting space.

Believe it or not, you can get a small humidor online at a website like CheapHumidors.com for just $10-20. There is a wide range of prices available if you're interested in buying used gear.

You can get a nicer or larger one for a bit more money, but you don't necessarily need to be ready to shell out hundreds of dollars. Humidors with minor cosmetic defects but perfect functionality typically sell for a discount, used or new.

If you had some cigars lying around before your investment in a

humidor, chances are they are really dry. Don't just toss them in the humidor; you need to progressively re-humidify them.

## SETTING UP YOUR HUMIDOR

You're definitely going to want a thermometer to put inside your humidor, as well as a hygrometer (that's an instrument that measures humidity, make sure it's a digital one; sometimes you might need to calibrate it so check the manual that comes with the device).

That way, you always know if your humidor is working at its ideal settings: try to keep the humidity between 68% and 72% and temperature at about 65-70° F.

To prepare your humidor, you'll need to complete a few steps.

First, prepare your humidifier; it's the device that is placed inside the humidor to keep the humidity level stable. Usually it will involve filling it with distilled water or propylene glycol, depending on the humidifier type.

Then you're going to want to wipe down the inside of the humidor with distilled water and wait about an hour for it to dry.

In the last preparation step you'll need to put a small glass of distilled water inside, along with your hygrometer and thermometer. Close the humidor and then leave the humidifier in there for 48 hours, adding more water if necessary, while the inner walls of the humidor are absorbing the moisture.

After this, your humidor should be operational, just watch the humidity level for a few days to make sure it stabilizes.

Remember, you need to let some fresh air in at least once every few weeks, but this is rarely a problem (except, perhaps, in winter). It may take some experimentation to decide what works best for you.

—Denis K.

# PLAZAS OF HAVANA

There's so much going on here that it took me countless visits and explorations through the years, with photos to go along with them, before I had a good understanding of all there is to see here. If you're not in a hurry, you could spend hours visiting the various buildings: Palacio de los Capitanes Generales, Castillo de la Real Fuerza, Palacio de los Condes de Santovenia (Hotel Santa Isabel), El Templete (church), and the Museo Nacional de Historia Natural. You can also take a stroll through the little park with its monument of Carlos Manuel de Céspedes in the center, visit the artists' studios above the restaurants (entrance on Oficios), or something I like to do…take a seat on one of the patios of those restaurants facing the plaza and watch the world go by while sipping on a mojito. Whatever it is that you may like to see or do, there's something here for everyone. One of my favorite restaurants is behind the square, facing the Havana Bay: El Templete Restaurant.

This is considered the oldest square in Havana, having been laid out in the 1520s soon after the city was established. But it wasn't until the late 1500s that it would be known as the Plaza de Armas. Due to the then colonial governor's (residing in the Castillo de la Real Fuerza) frequency of military exercises through the square, the people began calling it as it's known today. By the 18th century, the plaza was an important part of the workings of the city and something to behold, but over time it fell into decline. In 1935, projects were created to restore the plaza and return it to it's mid 1800s look. In 1955, some Cubans requested that the statue of Fernando VII in the center of the square be replaced with the one of Carlos Manuel de Céspedes that's there now.

The history of this square is rich, but it's also a beautiful place to visit, with all there is to see and do, starting with the book fair surrounding the little park (open Tuesday to Sunday) where they not only sell old books but trinkets of every sort...old Russian stuff like watches and cameras and all kinds of old Cuban stamps, posters, records, coins, and of course, books.

The Museo Nacional de Historia Natural wasn't my cup of tea, I prefer seeing Cuba's flora and fauna up close and personal. I loved the Palacio de los Capitanes Generales (give yourself an hour in this place) and enjoyed the Castillo de la Real Fuerza. I would have loved to be able to see more of the Hotel Santa Isabel but I couldn't get farther than the lobby...so far. The church was not what I expected. I could and I have walked around the park in the center and taken all kinds of pictures and had conversations with many people through the years.

One day I discovered the art galleries above the restaurants and have visited several times since then. The artists are quite approach-

able; naturally, they want to sell some art—it's allowed, legally, with papers. Angel Ramirez, one of my favorites, has his studio there, so does the famous female artist Zaida del Río. Sometimes the artists are there and sometimes they're not, but their art always is, and it costs nothing to look.

Finally, if you don't care for any of this stuff, at the very least you're going to enjoy sitting on one of the patios to have a cocktail or cafe con leche and watch locals and other tourists walk by. The fortress, palacio, church, and museum will all cost you a few dollars to enter and the palacio a couple more in order to be allowed to take pictures. It's a great spot to start or end your trip into Old Havana; taxis can stop alongside the plaza (via the Malecon) and are usually waiting to pick up a ride when you exit.

— M.S.

The Plaza de La Catedral is one of the most beautiful squares that I've had the pleasure of visiting in Cuba and I always make a point of visiting it at least once every trip. The Catedral de San Cristobal is the highlight and namesake of the square. Its original name is La Catedral de La Virgen Maria de La Concepcion Inmaculada de La Habana (that's a mouthful). Since being dedicated to San Cristobal its name changed to what it's known as today, Catedral de San Cristobal (and thank you for that). It was built by Jesuits on the site of another church in 1748-77. From this side of the square you're only about 100 meters from the Malecon. You can see it from the front of the church.

On the opposite side of the

63499. UN MULO DE LA HABANA.

Copyright, 1900, by Detroit Photographic

church is the building that has housed the Museo de Arte Colonial since 1963. The house was built in 1720 and was once the residence of Don Luis Chacon, the military governor of Cuba. The furniture housed within is a wonderful and extensive collection dating from the 18th-19th centuries, gathered from the great colonial mansions of Havana. It also includes some beautiful ceramics. Check it out even if it's only for the view you'll get from the upper level. It will make a great picture of the Catedral.

Jutting out from the side of the museum is a little dead end street called Callejon del Chorro. Right at the very end of the street is the Taller Experimental de Grafica. Created in 1962, it attracts many young artists and has become a meeting place for people in the arts. It's a workshop dedicating itself to the art of printmaking. Limited numbers of each print are made and some of the pieces are quite racy, taking jabs at the current political situation in Cuba. I was actually surprised that some of the stuff was allowed. It's definitely worth a visit. Just walk in and look

around. There's a whole bunch of pictures hanging on walls as soon as you walk in and you can see the presses a little further down. No one bothers you. The prices should be marked and are quite reasonable, if you wish to buy.

On one of the sides of the square you have the bar-restaurant El Patio and some souvenir shops. The restaurant has tables with umbrellas on the square as well as on a covered patio and indoors with an inner courtyard. I haven't had anything more than a cappuccino and cigar sitting at one of the tables on square, so I can't tell you about the food, but I wouldn't eat there. They always have a live band outside so it's a pleasant break after all that sightseeing. Beware, there will be someone wanting to do your caricature. Deal with it how you want; they're always pleasant. I have lots of them, anything you give them is appreciated.

Let's not forget the remaining side of the square, opposite the restaurant. In front of the Palacio de Lombillo (built in 1618) stands the statue of Antonio Gades, a famous flamenco dancer from Spain. He was born in 1936 and died in 2004. Why is this statue here? I have often wondered. He was a communist and defender of the Cuban Revolution. He had strong personal and political ties with Cuba. Fidel Castro was his best man when he married Marisol. He spent many of his latter years in Cuba and weeks before his death was presented with the order of Jose Marti by Fidel Castro. His ashes are kept at the National Pantheon of Heroes of the Revolution in Havana.

Well, that's about it. Give yourself more than an hour if you want to see it well, and a lot more than that if you want to relax with a coffee at the restaurant. I believe this to be one of the top three squares to visit in Havana.

— M.S.

## PLAZA SAN FRANCISCO

The Basilica and Monastery of San Francisco de Asis (where the Plaza gets its name) were built at the end of the 16th century but a square of some kind was here before that. It all started earlier that century when Spanish ships would stop on their way back to Spain. A market sprung up at that time, before the church, it was eventually moved to Plaza Vieja. Plaza San Francisco is the second oldest in the city. It has gone through some major restoration since the late 1990s. The Terminal Sierra Maestra, which faces the Plaza, is where the cruise ships unload all the tourists. The Lonja del Comercio was the old Commodities Market, built in 1909; it was part of the restorations that were done in 1996. It's now used as office space for foreign companies involved in joint ventures with Cuba.

The white marble fountain next to the church is called the Fuente de Los Leones (Fountain of Lions); it was carved by an Italian sculptor, Giuseppe Gaginni, in 1836. The statue in front of the entrance to the church is that of the Caballero de Paris. The statue was made by Jose Maria Lopez Lledin; it depicts a well-known, kind hearted street person who walked the length of Havana in the 50s, becoming quite famous.

The plaza faces the harbor and gives it a sense of being very large. It's a beautiful spot to have a drink on the patio of the Cafe Oriente, visit one of the art galleries, or enter the church and climb the bell tower for a fantastic view of the plaza and beyond. There's also a bank here where you can exchange money or get some from your credit card. This should be on the short list of places to visit in Old Havana, in my opinion.

— M.S.

# HOW TO SPOT
# FAKE CUBAN CIGARS

This chapter will help you tell fake Cuban cigars from the real thing.

One of the subjects I'm often asked about is, how to spot fake Cuban cigars. That's a good question, too, because despite the fact that Cuban cigars are still illegal for American cigar smokers to purchase, some choose to do it anyway. Is it because they're still considered "forbidden fruit," or is it that most cigar smokers believe Cuban cigars are still the world's best? It's more like a combination of the two; cigars made in Cuba are so great you just have to get your hands on some, even if it means risking losing them to U.S. Customs.

And they're not cheap, either; that is, unless you've been bamboozled by a hustler who will sell you a box of so-called "Havanas" at a great price while you're vacationing somewhere in the Caribbean. Chances are, they're fakes. What's that old saying? "A fool and his money…" More on that later.

Yes, at one time Cuban cigars actually were the best and had virtually no competition. Zino Davidoff realized this in the early part of the 20th century, and was one the first European retailers to introduce Cuban cigars to the world. Later, when he began producing cigars under his own name, they were made in Cuba. Additionally, when you see someone smoking a cigar in old movies from the 1920s to the 1960s (and very likely even after the 1962 embargo), you can bet they are smoking Cuban-made cigars.

## DON'T DO THE HUSTLE

What gets me is that, even though Nicaragua has been producing most of the world's best cigars of late, cigar smokers still jump at the chance to buy Cubans. Don't get me wrong. There are still some awesome cigars being made in Havana, but even there you'll find almost as many counterfeit Cuban cigars as the legit brands.

The streets are filled with hustlers looking for a mark to whom they can sell a box of genuine Cubans for a lot less than you'd pay in the store. The line these hustlers use to close the sale is usually something like, "My brother works in the Cohiba factory, yadda-yadda-yadda." The sucker, who thinks he is getting Cohibas or Montecristos is more likely getting cigars rolled with cheap tobacco that didn't even come from the genuine factory.

Since you're more likely to purchase fake Cuban cigars in places such as the Caribbean, the hustle goes something like this: The perp buys a bundle of cheapo, un-banded,

no-name brand cigars made in the Dominican Republic or elsewhere in Central America, sticks phony Cuban cigar bands on them, places them in a genuine Cuban box, and sells them to a sucker for as much as he can bleed him, often up to hundreds of dollars.

In both of the aforementioned cases, the mark doesn't realize he's been ripped off until he lights up one of his prized purchases. And if the mark is an experienced cigar smoker, he'll be even more livid that he allowed himself to be suckered. But enough about the hustle; let's get to the heart of how to spot fake Cuban cigars.

## CHECK THE PACKAGING

If the packaging looks suspicious, the contents probably are, too. Get to know how Cuban cigars are packaged, and you greatly reduce the chances of being ripped off. For example, the popular Cuban brands like Cohiba, Partagas, Punch, Hoyo de Monterrey, Romeo y Julieta, Montecristo, etc., all feature the Habanos S.A. seal on the top right-hand corner of the box. You also want to make sure the box has the Cuban warranty seal on the left side of the box. This is the familiar seal you see on all boxes of handmade cigars from Central America. They look a little like paper money and are printed in different colors. Of course, just about anything printed on paper can be reproduced, and with today's technology, it takes a really well trained eye to tell the difference. To help prevent this, in 2010 Habanos S.A. designed a new seal using watermarks, a super-strong adhesive, a hologram on the right side of the seal, and a barcode on the left.

Look for the Cuban seal of authenticity to help you avoid fake Cuban cigars.

If the hustlers are going through the trouble of counterfeiting the seals, you can bet the bands have also been faked. Just last year a customer sent me a box of counterfeit Arturo Fuente cigars (Dominicans!), and it was obvious the bands had been cheaply printed, most likely on a laser printer. Even the box was wrong, which I'll get to shortly. Though many fake Cuban cigar bands may look authentic—and in some rare cases are—it's not unusual to find bands with spelling errors, poor alignment, the wrong color and/or typeface, missing embossing, and in the case of Cohiba cigars, the wrong size or number of white squares on the band. The band is often the first place your eyes will go, so the more familiar you are with the genuine bands and their specific attributes, the sooner you'll know how to spot fake Cuban cigars.

Now, about that box of fake Fuentes. It had a glass top that slid in and out of the box. Fake Cohibas are often presented this way, too.

The fact is, the Cuban cigar industry doesn't make any cigar boxes with glass or even clear plastic tops. If someone tries to sell you a box of Cubans with a glass top, that alone should tell you to walk away.

One of the most important areas of the box to check is its bottom. A genuine box of Cuban cigars should have all of the following attributes:

The words "Habanos S.A., Hecho En Cuba"

If they're made by hand it will also say, "Totalmente a Mano" ("made totally by hand") rather than the more familiar "Hecho a Mano" as found on premium cigars handmade outside of Cuba.

A code for the factory where the cigars were made.

A date stamp that shows when the cigars were packaged.

Not unlike counterfeit cigar bands, the bottom of the box may be missing some of the above information, include typos, and may even be printed with different fonts.

## KNOW YOUR PRICES

Pricing can also be a tip-off to spotting fake Cuban cigars. If the price sounds too good to be true, it probably is. So get to know the relative prices on the top Cuban brands, especially the ones that are most often counterfeited like Cohiba Edición Limitadas, Montecristo No.2s, Partagas Serie D No.4s, etc. If someone tries to sell you a $350 box of Cubans for $50 or even $100, chances are they're not the genuine article.

Unless you've smoked a good number of genuine Cuban cigars it's easy to be fooled, especially if the counterfeiter got everything right except the cigars. This may present quite a dilemma since it's harder and more expensive—not to mention illegal—to get the real deal. So what can you do? There are certain attributes about Cuban cigars that differentiate them from non-Cubans. First, the feel and look of the cigar. Cuban wrappers tend to be naturally oily, have a smooth, buttery appearance, a uniform shade of brown that's unique to Cuban Corojo wrapper leaf, and except for figurados like Pyramids and Torpedoes, the caps are not as round on top. Cuban cigars also consistently produce grey ashes. A lot of cigars made outside of Cuba have similar attributes, but if the wrapper doesn't have that soft oily brown patina, the head is round, and the ash burns white, the tobacco is not of Cuban origin.

Suffice it to say: Caveat emptor mi amigos.

— Gary Korb, *Cigar Advisor*
(MAY 12, 2014)

# THE BURNING QUESTION: BURN ISSUES IN CIGARS

**P**remium cigars are a work of art. A hand-rolled cigar goes through many processes and many people will be involved in producing the fine smoke that you and I will eventually enjoy. Of course, not every cigar will attain the perfection that was intended by the team of people who produced it. The goal of this chapter is to try to help those who, like myself, want to know the reason for many common burn issues. Issues such as tunneling, canoeing, runners, and the many other issues we face from time to time.

Imagine yourself leaving work after a very long and stressful day. As you make your way home, you start thinking about a particular cigar you had your eye on over the last few days. This cigar may have been a gift by a dear friend, or even something you picked up on a whim. The closer you get to home the more your curiosity climbs until you finally decide that tonight you are going to light up that cigar and let your stress melt away.

As you walk through the door, there is complete silence. The kids are spending the night at a relative's house and your significant other isn't due home for a few more hours. You decide to take advantage of the quiet time and retrieve that special cigar.

As you nestle back into your smoking spot you begin to toast the foot of your cigar. Slowly the foot turns dark and smoke begins to float off of the burning end. After a few gentle puffs, your cigar is glowing cherry red and your stress begins to disappear.

The situation described above is a rarity for me, but I look forward to every chance I get to enjoy a fine cigar in a quiet and peaceful environment. A great smoke allows me to relax enough to forget about the stresses of the day and to enjoy some quality "me time."

While I am enjoying my quiet time with my cigar, I often get caught up in the way the cigar is burning. Lately I have been fascinated by the way my cigar burns and often wonder what makes my cigar burn even and under control sometimes, while at other times I experience a bad burning cigar.

As with any great hobby, I often find myself reading everything I can get my hands on, but when it comes to finding information on why my cigar is behaving the way it is, I am shocked at how difficult it is to find a specific reason for any given burn problem.

### PROPER LIGHTING TECHNIQUE

A bad burn has many different characteristics, the most common being a minor variation in the burn line. This generic form of a bad burn is characterized by a variation in the burn line of more than three eighths of an inch. This specific figure is used because an absolute perfect burn is an incredibly rare find in a hand rolled organic product such as a cigar. Often times a variation of under three eighths of an inch will correct itself and become more even over a short period of time.

Rushing through the initial lighting stages likely causes a bad burn line. The most critical part of cigar smoking is touching your preferred flame to the bare foot of your cigar for the first time.

Many times, an uneven burn can be avoided by simply taking care while toasting the foot of your cigar. To obtain a proper toast, hold your cigar between your thumb and middle finger while keeping the palm of your hand at a forty-five degree angle to the floor. With your opposite hand, ignite your lighter and slowly bring the flame closer to the foot of the cigar. As you slowly move the flame closer to the foot, watch for any discoloration or smoke coming from the foot of the cigar. Once the

foot of the cigar begins to emit a small amount of smoke, stop moving the flame towards your cigar. Usually, the flame tip will be just touching the foot or a slight distance away from the foot. Once the flame is at the correct distance from the foot, slowly begin rotating the cigar between your thumb and middle finger. This will help you to avoid overheating a single spot of the foot. (You may alternately choose to move the flame in a circular motion around the foot of the cigar.) As you rotate the cigar slowly, move the lighter with a minor wrist movement to evenly darken the foot of your cigar. You will know to extinguish your flame when the foot of the cigar is uniformly darkened and you have a thin glowing burn-ring around the foot portion of the wrapper.

Now that the cigar is properly toasted, place the head of the cigar in your mouth and repeat the toasting process as you take gentle puffs. Be sure to rotate the cigar in your mouth as you puff; this will help with an even light. When you feel that the cigar is evenly lit, remove it from your mouth and gently blow on the foot to see if you do, in fact, have an even burn around the rim of the foot. If the cigar is not evenly lit, place it back in your mouth and repeat the lighting process until you are satisfied with the burn. By taking the time to properly light your cigar you will greatly reduce the chances of encountering more severe burn issues.

## BURN PROBLEMS

In some cases, even after great care is taken to properly light your cigar, you will still develop burn problems with your cigar. One example of this would be an erratic burn due to wind. In most cases this is caused by smoking outdoors in windy conditions. As you puff on your cigar, wind blows along one side, which will cause increased combustion.

Another form of burn variation can be caused by uneven humidity throughout the cigar. Often times this happens when a naked cigar (one without cellophane) is placed directly against another surface that is moist or has increased humidity. As the wrapper comes into contact with this surface it acts much like sponge, pulling the extra moisture from the surface and wicking it into the inner tobaccos. When this cigar is lit, the more humid (i.e., moist) side of the cigar burns much slower than the dryer side. This causes a burn variation much like one caused by wind.

In some cases a burn problem can be the direct result of poor rolling. This type of problem is most common when cigars are rolled by apprentice rollers. These rollers may sometimes roll the tobacco too loose, or too tight, which will not only cause draw problems, but a variation in combustion. If this type of burn problem is suspected, pay close attention to the draw. If the draws seems to vary from tight to loose, or vice versa, the tobacco could be rolled poorly and result in uneven combustion.

These types of burn problems can sometimes be corrected by "touching up" the burn. Touching up a cigar is much like the initial toasting, but you only want to light the slow burning side of the cigar. If you take your time and avoid over puffing while touching up the burn, the slow burning side will begin to burn slightly faster. Over time, this can greatly increase the chances of the slow-burning side catching up with the fast side, thus correcting your burn problem. If you have a tight draw and/or a plugged cigar, you can often use cigar draw correction tools to restore a good draw.

At this point, you should feel confident in your ability to distinguish a good burn from a problematic one. In addition, you should feel comfortable in your ability to properly light a cigar and correct some of the more common burn problems.

## MORE SERIOUS BURN PROBLEMS

On occasion you may find yourself in a bit of a predicament due to a bad burn turning severe. Some of these severe burn problems can be prevented if caught early, but to catch one early, you must first understand what to look for and how to correct what you see.

### Canoeing

Of the severe burn problems, the most common is probably what is referred to as a "canoe" or described as "canoeing." This type of burn problem is when the burn line of your cigar gets out of control and burns deep into one side of the body. As shown in the photo below, you can see that it appears as though the cigar was split in half across the diameter, and only allowed to burn on one side.

A canoe can sometimes be caught early by paying attention to the appearance of the burn line. A proper burn line should be thin and even all the way around the circumference of the cigar. An early sign of the canoe is a burn line that becomes irregular and wide on one part of the cigar. This generally means that the cigar is heating up unevenly and there is a chance that one side will begin to combust at a faster rate. When this faster combustion occurs, the binder and wrapper will begin to burn away on the hotter side while

the burn remains slow on the opposing side.

To prevent a canoe in this type of situation, try slowing down your rate of smoking. Take extra care to puff lightly and less frequently. Doing this will allow the over-heated side of the cigar to cool which will, in turn, allow the burn to even up across the foot of the cigar. If the correction is slow going, you may want to consider touching up one side (as described previously) to accelerate the slower burning side of the cigar.

If you find yourself victim to a canoe that is too far-gone to correct by slowing down your rate of smoking, you can set the cigar down and allow it to go out. Once the cigar is cooled and completely unlit, use a guillotine style cutter to clip the foot of the cigar so that you have an even starting point

once again. Once clipped, place the cigar in your mouth and gently exhale through the cigar to help exhaust any foul chemical flavors that may be lingering due to partially combusted tobacco. After purging, begin the toasting and lighting process once again so that you may continue to enjoy your fine cigar.

## Tunneling

When tunneling occurs it can best be described as though a fuse was lit down the center of your cigar, burning away the core and leaving the exterior intact. The filler (or core) of your cigar is slowly burned from the inside out. As this tunneling occurs, the ash within the center falls out leaving what appears to be a hole or void within the body of your cigar.

This type of burn problem is common for slow smokers. When the cigar is left sitting in the ashtray, or not puffed frequently enough, the burning foot of the cigar partially goes out. As the outer part of the foot goes out first, the filler is left smoldering. The smoldering filler slowly continues

to burn throughout the length of the body. As more infrequent puffs are taken, the filler is kept lit while the binder and wrapper remain cool and unburned. Finally, when the smoker becomes bothered by the lack of smoke volume, the cigar gets tapped on the ashtray and the burned away filler falls, revealing a tunnel throughout the core of the cigar.

A common sign of this type of problem is a gradual lack of smoke while puffing. In addition to the lack of smoke, the ash will cease to progress down the cigar. To remedy a tunnel, the easiest thing

to do is immediately touch up the foot and begin to smoke at a slightly faster rate. A purge is also recommended at this point as the partially burnt tobacco may begin to leave an unenjoyable flavor on your palate.

Just like a canoe that is too far-gone, you can allow the cigar to cool and go out, then clip and re-light the foot to resume your smoke.

## Coning

"Coning" is the opposite of tunneling and presents itself as a sharp spike or peak protruding from the foot of the cigar. This is a burn problem that is common among those that enjoy smoking at an accelerated pace. As the cigar is puffed frequently, the dense filler begins to heat up and is not allowed adequate time to properly cool. As this happens, a sort of super heated bunch of filler burns the binder and wrapper away. Because this mass of filler stays hot and burns slower than its surrounding tobacco, it remains on the foot and protrudes away from the binder and wrapper. Of course, tobacco that is coarse, dense, and full of resins (like ligero)

will accentuate this problem since it does not burn as readily as other types of tobacco.

A common sign that coning may be occurring is a gradual harshness of the smoke. As the filler becomes overheated the tobacco surrounding it also becomes overly hot and has a tendency to produce hot and undesirable flavors.

Once it is determined that you are experiencing coning, it is recommended that the cigar be set down and allowed to cool for a few minutes. After the filler cools, smoking can resume, but be sure to resume at a much slower rate. This will allow the filler stay somewhat cool and catch up to the burn rate of the binder and wrapper.

Another way to help prevent coning is to allow the ash to remain on the foot of the cigar until it appears as though it is going to drop off. This will help to keep the foot cool by limiting airflow into the burning filler, which in turn slows down combustion.

## Runners

Of all the serious burn problems; "runners" have the most potential to destroy a cigar in a matter of minutes. When a runner occurs there is a dramatic change in the burn line and generally appears to take off down one part of the cigar.

In many cases, when a runner occurs it is due to a heavy vein in the wrapper. When this heavy vein begins to burn, it acts much like a fuse and begins to burn down the length of the cigar, destroying the wrapper as it burns. The best way to picture it would be to imagine unzipping your coat. As the zipper comes undone and travels down your coat, it moves in a predictable line and as it passes it opens the portion of the coat above it. In the case of the cigar the predictable path would be a heavy vein. As it burns down the vein, the wrapper pulls itself apart, leaving a large hole where the binder will begin to show.

Often times people will cat-egorize an off-center tunnel as a runner. In this case, a tunnel begins to form off-center and close to the wrapper of the cigar. As the tunnel worsens and the heat is increased, a hole will appear in your cigar, often times within an inch of the burn line. At first glance, this will appear as a small hole in the wrapper and will quickly progress into a much larger hole, resulting in the same effect as a runner. You will be left with a large opening in the wrapper exposing the binder and filler.

If you find yourself victim to a runner caused by a tunnel, the best course of action would be to let the cigar cool, then clip and re-light the cigar as mentioned above. If your runner is caused by a vein, the first thing to do is wet the tip of your finger and apply a small amount of saliva to the vein in question. This will help to slow

the exaggerated burn and hopefully stop it in its tracks. If the added moisture does not help, look to see if the vein shows any signs of getting smaller or stopping, if this is the case continue smoking with hopes that the runner will stop before destroying too much of your cigar.

It is often very difficult to tell if and when a runner will occur in a cigar. In fact, as I have been writing this article I have been smoking cigars with very large veins just so that I may possibly catch a picture of a runner in progress. I was unable to attain a picture of a runner, which simply goes to show that just because a cigar has large veins, there is no guarantee that they will cause burn problems.

You should now feel very comfortable diagnosing and dealing with burn problems ranging from simple to serious. The most important thing to remember when handling burn problems, regardless of their complexity, is to take your time in diagnosing and be patient when attempting to correct the issue at hand.

## NUISANCES WHILE SMOKING

Now that you have a grasp of what causes burn problems and how to correct them, I would like to briefly discuss a few burn nuisances. While these generally do not cause major problems, they can become increasingly irritating as they are experienced.

On occasion while smoking your cigar you may notice some bubbling or blistering at the burn line. While this generally does not lead to significant burn problems, it is an unattractive result of an over humidified cigar. When a cigar is over humidified the intense heat from the burning tobacco will sometimes flash-boil the excess humidity residing in your cigar. As this water turns into vapor it expands, causing the wrapper and binder to swell.

When the wrapper and binder begin to swell it causes a few different types of issues, the most common being small cracks in the wrapper due to the rapid expansion of the tobacco. This generally happens to tobacco that is fragile, such as a Cameroon wrapper leaf. When this type of expansion occurs in a wrapper that is a little tougher, such as Connecticut Shade, the leaf will expand but not crack. The result is minor bubbling or blistering of the tobacco.

The easiest way to correct a problem such as this is to slow down the rate at which you smoke. This will allow the excess moisture to turn to steam at a slower rate, which will ultimately cause the tobacco to swell slower.

Outside of cosmetic problems, an over humidified cigar can lead to your cigar being difficult to keep lit. For me personally, this is the most aggravating of the cigar nuisances. Due to the excess water residing in the cigar, the burn turns to a sort of smolder. This will lead to the tobacco constantly going out, especially if you slow your smoking rate to compensate for other problems such as cracking or blistering. There is nothing worse

than having to relight a cigar every few minutes or sucking the life out of it, just to keep it lit. To correct this type of problem you must pay very close attention to the burn line. Try to find the proper rate of smoking so that your cigar will stay lit and not damage the wrapper as it burns.

To avoid over humidified cigars, the best thing to do is to keep a watchful eye on your humidor's relative humidity level. By keeping your cigars at a constant relative humidity (%RH), in a range between 65–70%RH, you can solve many of these problems before they have a chance to develop.

Of course, it is possible that your cigar has been rolled with too much tobacco and has become tight or plugged, which will worsen the effects of excess humidity. In that case, you can often salvage a plugged or tight-drawing cigar by using a draw correction tool.

In the end, it may end up being less stressful and easier to simply pitch the cigar and grab a new one. However, the tips I have listed above may save you some aggravation and money by helping you to correct common burn issues and still enjoy your smoke.

## WRAPPING THINGS UP

First and foremost, I hope that you have enjoyed reading this as much as I enjoyed writing it. The purpose of taking the time to create a list of burn problems and fixes was due to the lack of resources I have found on the topic.

As a fairly new cigar enthusiast, I often found myself in search of answers to these burning questions. My results were often found in brief FAQ (Frequently Asked Questions) articles written by cigar retailers who did not spend much time discussing the problems I was experiencing. After hours upon hours of reading and researching cigars, I finally feel comfortable with diagnosing and correcting problems as I experience them. It is my intention to help those that find themselves in similar situations.

—Walt White

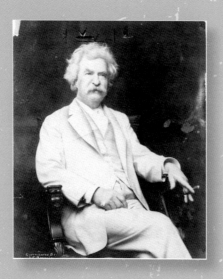

## ✮ MARK TWAIN HAD A GREAT SENSE OF HUMOR, ✮ BUT BAD TASTE IN CIGARS

"In a museum in Havana there are two skulls of Christopher Columbus—one when he was a boy and one when he was a man," Mark Twain once wrote of Cuba's capital city in *The Adventures of Thomas Jefferson Snodgrass*. Twain, known as an author, satirist, and American icon, was a champion of Cuban independence and also an avid and passionate cigar smoker.

In his 1897 travelogue *Following the Equator* (also known as *More Tramps Abroad)*, Twain mused, "I pledged myself to smoke but one cigar a day. I kept the cigar waiting until bedtime, then I had a luxurious time with it. But desire persecuted me every day and all day long. I found myself hunting for larger cigars...within the month my cigar had grown to such proportions that I could have used it as a crutch."

*My friends for some years now have remarked that I am an inveterate consumer of tobacco. That is true, but my habits with regard to tobacco have changed. I have no doubt that you will say, when I have explained to you what my present purpose is, that my taste has deteriorated, but I do not so regard it. Let me*

*tell you briefly the history of my personal relation to tobacco.*
*It began, I think, when I was a lad, and took the form of a quid,*
*which I became expert in tucking under my tongue. Afterward*
*I learned the delights of the pipe, and I suppose there was*
*no other youngster of my age who could more deftly cut plug*
*tobacco so as to make it available for pipe-smoking.*

*Well, time ran on, and there came a time when I was able to*
*gratify one of my youthful ambitions—I could buy the choicest*
*Havana cigars without seriously interfering with my income. I*
*smoked a good many…*

Twain was widely associated with cigar smoking. In his 1890s essay "Concerning Tobacco," Twain wrote the following:

"No one can tell me what is a good cigar—for me, I am the only judge. People who claim to know say that I smoke the worst cigars in the world. They bring their own cigars when they come to my house. They betray an unmanly terror when I offer them a cigar; they tell lies and hurry away to meet engagements, which they have not made when they are threatened with the hospitalities of my box."

# CUBAN RUM
# AND CIGARS

The largest portion of the world's rum production comes from the Caribbean and Latin America. It was for many years closely associated with Cuba. Rum is a distilled spirit made from sugarcane juice or sugarcane byproducts, such as molasses. The juice is fermented, and then distilled. Rum is most commonly made at approximately 80 Proof. The rums made from the sugarcanes of Cuba helped make fine rum world famous. Many famous producers today originated in Cuba, such as Bacardi.

Rum has an odd history. Mixed with beer or water to make grog, rum was among the engines of the British Royal Navy. It also fueled a number of pirate ships, where similar mixtures were referred to as bumbo.

And of course, like whiskey, it was a good in demand where trading was concerned, and became an important cog in the Triangluar Trade or the slave trade. It regained popularity during Prohibition, when rum runners brought Caribbean rums to American shores via clandestine night time off-shore deliveries.

Like the whiskey world, there are many kinds and grades of rum. White or light rums are among the

most popular commercial brands. They tend to be sweet, and are mainly used for making mixed drinks. But some dark or brown rums were aged in oak. And finally there are premium brown rums, aged in oak, that have much more in common with fine brandies, cognacs, or whiskeys.

Like whiskey and other potent potables, there is a market for the finer versions of this spirit. And it has its aficionados. It is this group we are interested in. Fine rum is an impressive drink. Firstly, they are made from molasses. Molasses makes the best, high quality rum. These rums are barrel aged, and can be served in brandy snifters or whiskey glasses. They are drunk neat or on the rocks. They give off impressive aromatics, filled with oak, stone fruits, raisin, honey, apricot, and honeysuckle, among others. They are not sweet, but rather, gorgeous elixirs.

For many years, there were varying traditions on what to sip while enjoying your cigar. Port? Brandy? Whiskey?

Winston Churchill was famous for liking brandy and

cigars. A frequent guest at Churchill's home Chartwell once remarked, "He is an exceedingly kind and generous host, providing unlimited Champagne, cigars, and brandy." One of his most famous biographers reported that Churchill always followed dinner with a cigar and a snifter or two of brandy, sometimes reading or writing until the wee hours of the morning.

Americans seemed to favor whiskey and cigars. Men like Ulysses S. Grant and Mark Twain made this combination famous. Mark Twain once quipped, "Too much of anything is bad, but too much good whiskey is barely enough."

But when in Cuba, savoring a fine Cuban cigar, the idea of sipping port, brandy, or whiskey is unthinkable. In Cuba you savor a fine, barrel-aged rum.

One of the most popular terms you will notice as you start investigating Cuban rum is the term "ron

añejo" which essentially means "old rum." That term seemingly indicates that this is a premiere product, though the degrees vary greatly from producer to producer.

Cuban rums have not been available in the United States since the early 1960s, but are available elsewhere around the world. And they are highly collectable. The fine rum market is vibrant and alive.

As these brands start to filter into the market, they will be easier to find and become more well known. But if you are lucky enough to travel to Cuba, these are some of the brands and rums you will want to sample.

So, sit back, pour two fingers of aged Cuban rum in a snifter or whiskey glass, and set it right down next to you as you begin to contemplate that Cuban cigar.

Here are some wonderful Cuban rums you should look for.

# ✳ TWO SPECIAL, RARE AGED CUBAN RUMS ✳

### RON EDMUNDO DANTES 25 YEAR OLD GRAN RESERVA

Ron Edmundo Dantes is among the highest quality rum brands today. The name of the brand comes from the famous novel by Alexander Dumas, *The Count of Monte Cristo.* This prestigious Cuban rum is made in Santiago de Cuba. They manufacture only 3,000 bottles annually. They produce two products: a 15 year old and a 25 year old rum. This 25 year old rum is golden in color, and known for it smooth taste with strong hints of vanilla. The 25 Year Old Gran Reserva bottle is decorated with 24 carat gold. The stylish package no doubt is reminiscent of the Montecristo cigar brand. However, do not be fooled. This is one of the most sought-after rums in the world. It is not to be confused with Montecristo rum, which is made in Guatemala. This bottle is very expensive and among the most difficult to find.

### HAVANA CLUB MAXIMO EXTRA ANEJO

Havana Club was founded by the Arechabala family in Cardenas, Cuba in 1878. They created the Havana Club brand in 1934. Havana Club is the largest producer of Cuban rum. Under the Pernod Ricard umbrella of brands, Havana Club is the fifth-largest rum brand in the world. The distillery now produces almost 4 million cases a year.  Maximo Extra Anejo is a non-vintage rum, but it is blended from a series of older rums, aged in oak casks. It is among the most expensive rums in the world. Oak, smokiness, vanilla, and caramel come across the nose with dried stone fruits. Hints of dark chocolate as well. Spicy finish. Fantastic.

## RON EDMUNDO DANTES 15 AÑEJO

From the famed small-production high-quality producer, Ron Edmundo Dantes, Extra Añejo 15 anos is the easier to find sibling to the famed 25 year old bottling. Smooth, elegant, with vanilla, stone fruit, and hints of tabacco. Lovely.

## HAVANA CLUB SELECCIÓN DE MAESTROS TRIPLE BARREL AGED RUM

This is Havana Club's Cuban Barrel Proof edition. It's 45% more powerful than their other less expensive editions. It is the result of an extraordinary collaboration between the members of the Maestros Roneros Guild of Cuba, led by the talented Don Jose Navarro, and Havana Club.

The casks were hand-picked by the maestros roneros from the company's finest aged stocks. The rums selected by the maestros roneros are finished in special casks chosen for their aromatic properties. A big, impressive rum, with honey and apricot and power to boost! Exceptional.

## RON VARADERO ANEJO 15 AÑOS

Ron Varadero was founded in 1862 with the support of the Spanish crown. The name comes from the town in the northern part of Cuba. Varadero is the second largest producer of rum in Cuba after Havana Cub. This golden rum is aged 15 years in white American oak casks. The nose comes up with big whiffs of vanilla and brown sugar and figs. It has a beautiful, intense, long finish. Highly prized.

## HAVANA CLUB GRAN RESERVA AÑEJO 15 AÑOS

This rum is created by continually blending selected aged rums and aguardientes. Many of them are in old oak casks. Beautiful hints of vanilla and dried stone fruits on the nose, with hints of honey. Toasty with a lovely vanilla note to savor at the end. Among one of the best aged rums in Cuba.

## RON CUBAY 10 YEAR OLD

Ron Cubay was founded in 1964 in Santa Dominco, Villa Clara, and is often referred to as "The Taste of the Center." This brand was only meant for local consumption, but its reputation grew as such that it was eventually made available on the international market in 2010. Aged 10 years in barrel, this is an incredibly smooth rum, with great character and flavor. The nose exhibits honey, brown sugar, and vanilla with hints of apricot. Caramel and vanilla come across the palate. Ends dry and the vanilla lingers.

## RON MULATA 15 YEAR OLD

Ron Mulata is one of seven products produced by Tecnoazucar. This is an excellent example of Cuban rum. This is a blend of 15 year old rums matured in 180 liter American oak casks. This is an exceptional rum made with finesse. Lovely vanilla and stone fruits. Very sophisticated.

## RON SANTIAGO DE CUBA 12 YEAR OLD

This 12-year-old aged rum is made in Santiago, Cuba. Aged in oak casks, the rum is dark in color and has notes of vanilla, oak, and other spicy notes. Hints of dark chocolate, caramel, smoke, and brown sugar. Dark, rich, and well-reviewed, this rum has won over curious tasters. Sophisticated. Complex.

## RON VIGIA GRAN RESERVA 18 AÑOS

This is a rum made in the classic aged essence, having been matured in oak casks for 18 years. But the difference here is that Ron Vigia is not made from molasses but from sugar syrup, which apparently, according to some authorities, produces a lighter style aged rum. Nevertheless, experts agree, that this aged rum is worth trying, and a very good entry in the field. Floral and hints of stone fruits and vanilla.

Several European distillers have taken Cuban-made rums and aged and bottled them, releasing them into the marketplace. Here are a few examples of high-end, high-quality rums.

### SANCTI SPIRITUS 14 YEAR OLD

This is bottled by English whiskey producer Duncan Taylor. This 14-year-old rum is aged in oak but Sancti Spiritus is special—it is among the only single barrel aged rums in the world. This is a very limited bottling. Less than 250 bottles. A unicorn aged rum. Highly prized.

### SANCTI SPIRITUS 14 YEAR OLD

This is oak aged Cuban rum from the Sancti Spiritus distillery. It is bottled by one Scotland's oldest independent bottlers, WM Cadenhead, founded in 1842. This cask-strength rum is golden in color, and features stones fruits and vanilla. Extraordinary.

### LA COMPAGNIE DES INDES CUBA 16 YEAR OLD VINTAGE

Compagnie Des Indes is a French company founded by Florent Beuchet, whose family owns the Emile Pernot Absinthe Distillery. Beuchet bottles different blendings to make high-end, high-quality rums from around the Caribbean. He has bottled many vintages of aged Cuban rum. They are exquisite in their character and the reviews from many of the rum aficionados have been incredible. Any one of his Cuban rum bottlings is well worth seeking out and trying.

Havana Club 5 Añejo Especial
Havana Club Añejo 7
Ron Varadero Añejo 7 Años
Ron Mulata Añejo 7 Year Old

## BACARDI AND CUBA

Bacardi was the first and most well known rum sold worldwide in the modern era. Though it is no longer manufactured in Cuba, a history of Cuban rum would be incomplete without it. Bacardi Limited is currently one of the most famous spirits brands in the world—and it is among the largest family-owned, privately-held spirits companies. The brand was made famous by their Bacardi white rum.

Don Facundo Bacardí Massó, a Spanish wine merchant born in Spain, emigrated to Cuba in 1830. In those days, rum was not a refined drink, and often made with low standards for local consumption. It was Facundo who began systematizing the process, creating a proprietary strain of yeast to make the base product from which the rum was distilled. Facundo was also credited with aging rum in white oak barrels to mellow the final product. This is how he manufactured the first clear, or "white," rum in the world.

Facundo, and his brother José, first established the distillery in Santiago de Cuba in 1862. Bats soon made their home in the far recesses of the factory, and the instantly recognizable bat logo was born. Emilio Bacardi, Facundo's eldest son, was appointed Mayor of Santiago de Cuba in 1899 by U.S. General Leonard Wood, after the Cuban war for independence from Spain during the turn of the last century. Emilio had been a leader in the Free Cuba movement. How-

ever, after the Castro Revolution the Bacardi family fled, and ever since, Bacardi rum has been made elsewhere. However, the label still states: "Company founded in Santiago de Cuba in 1862."

The most famous symbol of rum's rise in Cuba is the Bacardi Building, which is still considered one of the crowning achievements in Cuban architecture. As the company became more international in scope, with offices around the world, a new main office befitting their world status was built in 1930, as the third generation entered the business. The executives "branded Cuba as the home of rum, and Bacardi as the king of rums." The headquarters, as it still stands today, became known as the "Cathedral of Rum." The Bacardi Building in Havana is regarded as one of the finest Art Deco buildings in Latin America.

— Carlo DeVito

Hemingway sitting by the pool at Finca Vigía, his home in San Francisco di Paula, Cuba (Ernest Hemingway Collection. John F. Kennedy Presidential Library and Museum, Boston)

## ⚹ HEMINGWAY IN CUBA ⚹

Ernest Miller Hemingway was one of the most famous American novelists, short story writers, and journalists of the 20th century. His clean, lean prose style influenced generations of writers. He was a well-traveled, well-known outdoor sportsman, and among the most famous literary celebrities of the 20th century. His novels include *The Sun Also Rises* (1926), *A Farewell to Arms* (1929), *For Whom the Bells Tolls* (1940), and *The Old Man and the Sea* (1952). His short stories include *The Snows of Kilimanjaro, The Killers, A Clean Well-Lighted Place,* and many others. He won the Nobel Prize for Literature in 1954.

Hemingway lived on a plantation he called *Finca Vigía,* or "Lookout Farm," in San Francisco de Paula, Cuba, from mid-1939 to 1960. He rented it at first. After he married his third wife, journalist Martha Gelhorn, he bought the small 15-acre farm and house outright in December 1940 for $12,500.

Hemingway wrote most of his famous Spanish Civil War novel, *For Whom the Bell Tolls*, while living at *Finca Vigia*. He also wrote *The Old Man and the Sea* while at *Finca Vigia*.

Hemingway was one of Cuba's most internationally famous residents. He was known to stay out late drinking in the many saloons. Especially endearing to the Cuban people was the fact that, even after the Cuban revolution in early 1959, Hemingway retained good relations with the Cuban government, and remained a resident until 1960, a year after Castro took power and a year before Hemingway took his own life. While still a resident, Hemingway presented a trophy to Fidel Castro who won a fishing contest in 1960, which was named in Hemingway's honor.

After Hemingway committed suicide in Idaho on July 2, 1961, the house became the property of the Cuban people.

In the intervening years, *Finca Vigia,* which remained a popular icon in modern Cuban history, fell into disrepair. But the Cuban government refurbished the estate in 2007. Hemingway remained a popular icon in Cuba. He has a lasting reputation for being a champion of Cuban life as well as its drink.

"Don't bother with churches, government buildings or city squares, if you want to know about a culture," Hemingway once wrote. "Spend a night in its bars."

Hemingway was a fan of mojitos and daiquiris. His quote can still be found engraved at renowned bar La Bodeguita del Medio where he carved it himself. It was the drinking establishment where Hemingway imbibed his first mojito. "My mojito in La Bodeguita, My daiquiri in El Floridita."

An authentic mojito is usually made with Cuban rum, lime juice, mint leaves, and a splash of sparkling water. But at La Bodeguita, Hemingway had his own version, which substituted sparkling wine for the club soda.

## HEMINGWAY'S MOJITO

*1 lime*

*2 tsp. natural cane sugar*

*5 fresh mint leaves*

*1.5 oz. Cuban rum*

*3 oz. sparkling wine*

1. Juice the lime.
2. Then add juice, sugar, and mint leaves to a rocks cocktail glass.
3. Muddle the mint leaves.
4. Add rum and sparkling wine. Stir slowly.
5. Garnish with lime twist.

Hemingway's favorite Cuban bar for the daiquiri was called El Floridita. It was known for their version of a Hemingway Daiquiri, also known in-house as a Papa Double. It was a double of the Hemingway version of a daiquiri.

## PAPA DOUBLE

*1 lime*

*½ grapefruit*

*Ice*

*3.5 jiggers Bacardi white rum*

*½ oz. Maraschino liqueur*

1. Extract juice of lime and grapefruit into a glass.
2. In a blender place shaved ice, rum, liqueur, and juices.
3. Blend on high until frothy.
4. Pour into a large glass.
5. Garnish with lime.

# CUBA LIBRE

The Cuba Libre was invented by Americans who brought Coca-Cola with them on their expeditions into Cuba either during the Spanish-American War, or the occupation thereafter. This was their version of a highball. The phrase "Cuba Libre" means Free Cuba, and was coined during the turn of the previous century to popularize Cuba's shaking off the colonial yoke of Spain rule. Ever since, the Rum and Coke drink has been a popular favorite.

*1 lime*
*1 shot rum*
*1 12-oz. cola*

**1.** In a Tom Collins glass filled with ice, squeeze the juice of one lime.
**2.** Add rum.
**3.** Pour enough cola to fill the rest of the glass.
**4.** Garnish with a lime twist.

ESTAURANTE
BAR

ridita

A DEL DAIQUIRI

# CATALOG OF CUBAN CIGAR MANUFACTURERS

# BOLÍVAR

## STRENGTH: FULL

Founded by José F. Rocha in 1902, the Cuban Bolívar has a reputation among cigar aficionados of being one of the biggest, boldest, and most full-bodied cigars. The cigar was named after Simón Bolívar, a formidable political and military leader of the nineteenth century who helped establish independence for many South American countries, ending much of the colonial rule established by the Spanish monarchy.

So when and how did the major export brand, Bolívar, gain worldwide popularity? After Rocha's death in 1954, the company along with the company's name rights were purchased. The new owner, Cifuentes y Cia, relocated production to the world-renowned Partagás Factory in Havana. Today the factory is named the Francisco Pérez Germán Factory, and it has subsequently been moved to a new location.

## CIGARS

- Belicosos Finos
- Coronas Gigantes
- Coronas Junior
- Petit Coronas
- Royal Coronas
- Tubos No. 1 Tubos
- Tubos No. 2 Tubos
- Tubos No. 3 Tubos

# ★ BOLIVAR SUPER CORONAS EDICION LIMITADA 2014 ★

This was the last of the three Edición Limitadas of 2014 that I tried and I have to say, 2014 was one of the best years, if not the best year, of Edición Limitada releases, and this Bolívar is no exception. I expected to find this cigar and the other two while I was in Havana this 2014 but none of them were available. What I had discovered since coming back is that you can find them pretty much everywhere else on the planet, including in Canada. Of course, they're not sold at Cuban prices.

This cigar weighs in at 48 x 140 (5.5"), making it a Grand Corona. It was released in late 2014 (depending on where you live) in boxes of 25 cigars.

This cigar has a dark wrapper and is kind of bumpy all over, the cap included. It's hard to the touch, with a couple of soft spots. The pre-light draw gave me light cedar; the draw was excellent even after lighting. Once lit, there was big wood and earth, with chocolate undertones. Off the hop, I have to say this seemed like it was going to be a wonderful smoke. The burn was a bit off as I reached the first inch and it turned out to be a medium- to strong-bodied smoke.

Nearing the half, I flicked the ash so it didn't drop on my friend's floor,

only to have it drop on its own a half-inch later. (That was odd.) This cigar, so far, has been a great smoke, with very Bolívar-like flavors. Most of the Regionals and Edición Limitadas cigar brands that are used for these cigars don't follow their usual signature *ligas* (blends).

The burn straightened itself out before reaching the half, but now past the half it's off again so I touch it up this time. It pretty much maintains this flavor profile all the way through, with hints of toasted coffee bean and dark chocolate creeping in now and then.

It got a little bitter and stronger during the last quarter, and at one point I flicked the ash because I can see it's burning hotter through the middle. It had gone out by then so I did a relight. I'm still able to smoke it until I can't hold it any longer. That last piece surprised me—I thought after that relight it would have been bitter, but the flavor remained the same. That's incredible for such a young cigar.

In conclusion, I have to get myself some and I would recommend the same for you. Although they claim the leaf in this cigar has been aged two years (which allows it to be remotely approachable), it still needs some time to age. This is going to be an exceptional smoke a couple of years down the road. —M.S.

# COHIBA

## STRENGTH: MEDIUM

Cuban Cohibas, famously known as Fidel Castro's preferred smoke, have held the reputation of being made from the finest cigar tobacco available in Cuba. The cigar was delivered to the world in 1966 as Havana's premier brand and maintains an association with extravagance and refined taste. It started when one of Fidel Castro's bodyguards shared his own personal stash of cigars that had been hand made for him by Eduardo Rivera, a local artisan. Castro was so pleased that he orchestrated a special production of this unbranded blend. They were manufactured under the strictest security for Castro (who has not smoked now for more than a decade) and other top government officials.

Cohiba is derivative of the Taino Indian word for "tobacco." However, Cohiba is scrupulous about choosing tobacco for its cigars. While it is pulled from the fields in San Luis and San Juan y Martinez zones in the Vuelta Abajo region of Pinar del Río Province, Cohiba's tobacco must be picked from the Vegas Finas de Primera, meaning first-class tobacco fields (the location of which Cohiba keeps occult). For example, in 1992, only ten tobacco fields from 700 acres were chosen to make Cohiba cigars.

> "Before the distinctive black-and-yellow band of the Cohiba became a badge of plutocracy, it was the favored smoke of Cuba's revolutionary elite [...] Soon these long, elegant cigars became as much a part of the revolutionary look as facial hair and military fatigues, thanks to Che Guevara's pronouncement that he had never smoked a better cigar."
>
> —Newsweek

**COHIBA**

*Habana, Cuba*

**COHIBA**

Habanos
DENOMINACIÓN DE ORIGEN PROTEGIDA

**ESTE PRODUCTO PUEDE SER DAÑINO PARA SU SALUD Y CREA ADICCION.**

**MINSAP**

# ✴ COHIBA ROBUSTOS SUPREMOS ✴
## EDICION LIMITADA 2014

I had originally smoked one of these cigars (unbanded) a few months before they were released and really enjoyed it. The one I smoked for this review was gifted to me by a friend, and I was anxious to try it. I actually enjoyed the unbanded one more, it was fresher. The one I smoked for this review was undergoing some kind of change; it definitely needed some time before being smoked now.

This cigar weighed in at 58 x 127 (5") and is considered a Robusto. It had a dark, bumpy wrapper that is oily and slightly mottled. Cut and lit, it had a good draw, with flavors of wood and chocolate and with a hint of floral. It was very different than the fresher one I smoked, the initial flavors on this one had settled down, but I predict that these cigars are going to go through many more changes before they're ready to be smoked.

Right from the start the burn was already off, and so it went pretty much through the entire smoke. Less than an inch through the cigar and wood overpowered all other flavors and the hints of floral were gone. At the one-inch mark the cigar became very earthy, with wood taking a back seat. At this point, it was a medium- to full-bodied cigar.

One-third into the cigar, the burn was worse and the touch of floral reared its ugly head once again. Nearing the half and the ash was still holding on. I took off one of the bands without upsetting the ash but at about the halfway mark it fell on its own. I started picking up some maduro-like flavors, earthy with floral undertones. It turned out to be a full-bodied smoke. I took the second band off and the burn was so bad that I needed to do a touch-up. The cigar was very full-flavored and getting stronger. By the time I got to the last third the cigar became unsmokable for me.

As I said, the cigar needs some time to rest —it's only going to get better with age. If you can still find them, they're worth buying.

The company's origin is a mansion outside of Havana, called the El Laguito Factory, where they produced all the Cohiba cigars. In 1961, a cigar-rolling school for women was established there, and only later it became home to the Cohiba brand. Cohiba cigars owe their smooth flavor to a unique (among Cuban brands) third fermentation process done in the factory's wooden barrels.

With the guidance of Cubatabaco, the Cuban state tobacco-marketing bureau, the Cohiba brand was officially launched in 1968. Avelino Lara, the head of the El Laguito Factory, was asked by Cubatabaco to create a new super-premium blend. In the beginning, only a few thousand boxes of Cohibas were produced each year.

Cohibas gained fame after they were given as diplomatic gifts. The brand eventually reached cult status among aficionados but they were not commercially for sale to the public until 1982. In 1992, Cuba exported approximately 60 million cigars and approximately 3.4 million of those cigars bore the Cohiba label.

## SPECIAL RELEASES

Habanos S.A. launched the Cohiba Línea 1492 in 1992, in honor of Christopher Columbus and his voyage to the Americas in the year 1492. Each cigar was named for a century since the discovery of the Americas, and are in different sizes. The initial launch included the Siglo I, Siglo II, Siglo III, Siglo IV, and Siglo V, with a Siglo VI introduced in 2002.

During the annual Habanos Festival, as well as brand anniversaries, Cohiba offers limited-releases of cigars. There is also the annual Edición Limitada cigar. Relatively new (2007) is the Maduro 5. This maduro-wrapped Cohiba is available in three sizes.

# CIGARS

- Behike BHK 52
- Behike BHK 54
- Behike BHK 56
- Coronas Especiales
- Espléndidos
- Exquisitos
- Genios Maduro 5
- Lanceros
- Magicos Maduro 5
- Panetelas
- Piramides Extra
- Robustos
- Secretos Maduro 5
- Siglo I
- Siglo II
- Siglo III
- Siglo IV
- Siglo V
- Siglo VI

## CUABA

### HABANA · CUBA

ESTE PRODUCTO
PUEDE SER DAÑINO
PARA SU SALUD Y
CREA ADICCION.

MINSAP

**Habanos**
DENOMINACIÓN DE ORIGEN PROTEGIDA

HABANA

HABANA·CUBA

REPUBLICA DE CUBA

# CUABA

## STRENGTH: MODERATE TO BOLD

The Cuaba brand was introduced in November 1996, to a ballroom full of tuxedo-clad revelers in the Claridge's Hotel in London, by Habanos president Francisco Linares. The line was an attempt to revive *figurados*, the irregularly-shaped cigars known to be more difficult to manufacture but of distinct quality, which had initially been very popular in the early twentieth century but were in decline since about the 1930s. It was an all-perfecto line of cigars, being of even length and even gauge.

At the launch, Carlos Izquierdo González, the brand's originator, and a team of a dozen or so highly skilled *torcedores* (cigar rollers) hand-rolled *figurado* cigars before invited guests and media. When first introduced, the Cuaba were hand-rolled without the use of a press, and thus, the original Cuabas were of differing sizes, like the historic *figurados*, even within the same box. A year later, after molds, to more or less standardize size and shape, were finally created, the original Cuabas became great collectors' items.

Even with molds, Cuabas are still somewhat irregularly shaped cigars. They are pointed at both ends, the style that made Havana world famous at the end of the 19th century.

The cigars are produced using only Grade 7 rollers. The blend used to make these cigars was aimed at emulating the Montecristo profile. The tobacco comes from the Vuelta Abajo (Pinar del Río).

# CIGARS

- Distinguidos
- Divinos
- Exclusivos
- Salomónes

# ✱ DISCONTINUED ✱ BRANDS

Pre- and Post-revolution Cuba has seen a number of brands discontinued over the years. Here is a short and quite possibly incomplete list of the brands that could be identified via a search of various records. Post revolution brands include: Cabañas, Caney, Cifuentes, Davidoff, Dunhill, Gispert, La Corona, La Escepción. La Flor del Caney, Los Statos de Luxe, María Guerrero, and Siboney.

Several websites contain lists of brands that were discontinued for various and sundry reasons before the revolution. There are more than 1700 registered cigar manufacturers whose brands are no longer active or discontinued.

## ✱ DAVIDOFF ✱
### THE MOST COLLECTED DISCONTINUED BRAND

Davidoff Cuba cigars are both smooth and prized, being only made from 1968 to 1992. Some Cuban Davidoffs may be found in private stashes today, but are closely held by collectors.

Though the Davidoff name has been famous in the cigar industry for more than a century, the actual Cuban brand was a relatively recent venture. Davidoff was one of the most successful cigar stores in the world. In 1967, Cubatabaco, the Cuban state tobacco conglomerate created by the Castro government to oversee the Cuban cigar industry, approached Zino Davidoff and his management about creating a line of cigars just for his shops, that would bear his name. The first cigars were released the following year.

Around that time, Castro's own private cigars, Cohiba, also came into existence. They were made at the new El Laguito cigar factory in

Havana. Davidoff cigars were also hand rolled there. The first cigars introduced included the No. 1, the No. 2, and Ambassadrice (which all shared the same sizes as the early Cohiba line) and the Châteaux Series. The 1970s saw two more series added to the line, the milder Mille Series and the Dom Pérignon series, an *homage* to the world famous champagne. To commemorate Zino's 80th birthday, a new series, the Anniversarios, was introduced in 1986.

Zino Davidoff was born in Novhorod-Siverskyi, Ukraine on March 11, 1906. He father, Henri Davidoff, was a successful tobacco merchant in Kiev. Zino, the eldest son, fled Russia with his parents and half his family in 1911, relocating to Geneva, Switzerland. Henri opened another cigar store there in 1912. To learn more about the tobacco trade, Zino traveled to Argentina, Brazil, and finally Cuba in 1924. He stayed in Cuba for two years working at a plantation. He returned six years later to Geneva, where he took over his father's business.

Spared the destruction of the war, Switzerland, a neutral country during World War II, became a haven for wealthy Europeans. These were boom for the small tobacconist. Zino greatly expanded the store's offerings and business.

It was during this time that Zurich cigar company A. Durr Co. successfully launched the Hoyo de Monterrey Châteaux Series of Cuban cigars inspired by the wines of Bordeaux. Zino helped to make the brand a resounding success. Zino also became a successful author, publishing several books on Cuban cigars. He may have invented, around this time, the first desktop humidor.

By the time Zino sold his store in Geneva to the Max Oettinger Company, it was considered the premiere cigar store in the world. Oettinger had been founded in 1875, and was one of the first importers of Cuban cigars in Europe, dominating the markets in France, Germany, and Switzerland. Oettinger paid the then unheard of sum of $1 million in 1970. Zino stayed active on Davidoff's behalf, acting as spokesperson and brand ambassador until his death at 87 years of age in 1994.

Davidoff stopped selling Havana Davidoffs in December 1992, after Davidoff and Cubatabaco announced in a press release in December 1991, "There will not be any more Davidoff cigars manufactured in Cuba or using Cuban tobacco, and the Davidoff Havanas will only be available until exhaustion of existing stocks, and in any event, not later than the end of 1992."

## CIGARS

The cigars within the Cuban Davidoff line included:

| | |
|---|---|
| No. 1 | Château Margaux |
| No. 2 | Château Mouton Rothschild |
| Ambassadrice | Château Yquem |
| Tubo | |
| Dom Pérignon | **MILLE SERIES** |
| | 1000 |
| **CHÂTEAUX SERIES** | 2000 |
| Château Haut-Brion | 3000 |
| Château Lafite | 4000 |
| Château Lafite-Rothschild | 5000 |
| Château Latour | |

# DIPLOMATICOS

## STRENGTH: MODERATE

Released in 1966, Diplomaticos was the first brand of Cuban cigars to be released in post-revolutionary Cuba that was offered to the public within Cuba and internationally. The Cohiba was the very first cigar brand created post-Revolution, but was solely used for private consumption by Castro and as diplomatic gifts.

The original concept behind Diplomaticos, was to offer a "value" Montecristo. The Diplomatico brand was specifically marketed to French cigar consumers. Like the Montecristo line, Diplomaticos offered five handmade numbered sizes. Ten years after the introduction of Diplomaticos in 1976, the No. 6 and No. 7 were introduced to the line, again emulating Montecristo's Especial No. 1 and Especial No. 2. However, they were phased out by the mid-1980s.

The Diplomaticos line was manufactured at the Jose Marti factory, where almost all Montecristo cigars are made. The factory no longer exits today. Montecristo and Diplomaticos are made using a similar blend of tobaccos. However, Diplomaticos are meant to be offered at a more affordable price and offer a slightly milder smoke.

 CIGARS

- No. 2

Habanos

D.O.P.

DENOMINACIÓN DE ORIGEN PROTEGIDA

WARNING
**TOBACCO SMOKE HURTS CHILDREN**

Tobacco smoke can trigger asthma attacks in children.

Health Canada

AVERTISSEMENT
**LA FUMÉE DU TABAC NUIT AUX ENFANTS**

La fumée du tabac peut provoquer des crises d'asthme chez les enfants.

Santé Canada

DIPLOMATICOS

HABANA

CIGARS · CIGARES

REPÚBLICA DE CUBA

Sello de garantía nacional de procedencia

# ✦ DIPLOMATICOS PETIT ROBUSTO ✦
## EDICION REGIONAL ESPANA 2012

I love this size, 50 x 102 (4"), just a hair smaller both in ring gauge and length than the Petit Edmundo. Five thousand numbered boxes of ten cigars were released in 2012. I know many people who have bought these cigars, one of which sent me a couple. It's a great cigar for the size, to smoke when you either don't have a lot of time or when you want to smoke several (as in my case) cigars within a certain period of time. This cigar was hard to the touch with a flawless construction and a slightly bumpy cap. The pre-light draw was big on cedar. Once lit, the draw was a little firm but not too bad. I picked up a touch of earthiness, wood, and a hint of floral notes. The burn looked like it was going to be off, but it corrected itself after the first half-inch.

I tasted more earth than wood and it gave me the impression that the profile is somewhat like a regular production Diplomatico, which is great for my taste. They don't make enough Diplomatico vitolas but my guess is that not enough of us buy them…supply and demand. The draw gave me just a bit of resistance but it only meant I had to slow down my smoking so as not to overheat the cigar.

By the time I reached the first quarter, the burn was off and the cigar was earthy, musty, and picked up strength. At the halfway mark the ash fell on its own and, just so you know, the floral notes were still existent. I didn't care for the floral. The flavors really didn't change too much, and midway through it turned out to be a medium-strong cigar. The burn was still off and I couldn't resist, I touched it up with my torch as I neared the last quarter. I finally had to let it go when it became difficult to hold.

I smoked this cigar a year ago at a picnic on a long weekend. I wish I could have given it more attention but after all is said and done, it wasn't that complicated a cigar. Rather easy to smoke with not a lot of changes. It could use a bit of age and I'm sure one year will make a big difference for this cigar. It's worth a try if you get the opportunity.

—M.S.

# EL REY DEL MUNDO

## STRENGTH: LIGHT TO MEDIUM

These cigars are named "The King of the World" for a good reason. This brand of premium quality and highly-priced cigars appeared in 1882 from the Antonio Allones factory.

Habanos S.A. has identified El Rey Del Mundo as a local brand. It is a small producer inside Cuba, with small market share. The line is made up of light to medium strength cigars. The tobacco is sourced from the premium Vuelta Abajo region. Special Releases commenced in 1999 with the inclusion of El Rey del Mundo cigars in the Siglo XXI Humidor.

## CIGARS

- Choix Suprême
- Demi Tasse

# FONSECA

**STRENGTH: MILD**

Famously dashing and impeccably groomed, Don Francisco E. Fonseca founded his namesake cigar company. He was born around 1869 or 1870 in Manzanillo, Cuba. In 1892, Fonseca established a factory in Havana and created his own cigar brand, which he officially registered in 1907. Fonseca became an American citizen in 1895, and in 1903, Fonseca and his wife, Teresa Boetticher de Fonseca, immigrated to New York. Fonseca operated cigar factories in New York City and Havana and regularly traveled to and from Cuba to run F.E. Fonseca Fábrica de Tabacos y Cigarros. This dual citizenship was evident in his business stationery, which depicted both the Statue of Liberty and the Morro in Havana.

Spanish poet Federico García Lorca was fond of cigars. In his writings, he identified the Fonseca brand, writing of the "blond head of Fonseca" (*la rubia cabeza de Fonseca*), along with "the pink of Romeo y Julieta" in his poem "Son de Negros en Cuba," from his book *Poet in New York,* published in 1940.

# ✦ FONSECA NO. 4 EDICION REGIONAL BENELUX 2010 ✦

I've always liked the look of a Fonseca, with its tissue wrapping. The one with the double bands looked even nicer. What they lack in complexity they make up for in presentation. The vitola is called a Hermosos No. 4, which is a Corona Extra at 48 x 127 (5"). Sixteen hundred boxes of twenty-five were made and released in 2010 for the Belgium, Netherlands, and Luxembourg markets.

When I unwraped this cigar it didn't look very pretty. It was dry and bumpy, in a toffee-colored wrapper with no veins and with what seemed like little bits of the tissue remaining on the cigar. The cigar was hard to the touch with very little to no give. The pre-light seemed promising, however, with big cedar flavors that came through.

Once lit, it was a perfect draw. By the time I got to the first half-inch I could see the burn was already a bit off. It was a little salty with cedar notes and was mild- to medium-body in strength. By about the first inch

the burn was still a bit off but not long after that it straightened itself out. It remained woody with a hint of nuttiness.

The ash fell on its own at about the halfway mark. It hit the floor with a thud. It was a good solid ash that didn't disintegrate when it hit the floor. The flavors didn't change much at this point; it maintained the same woodiness with a hint of herbal flavor. A mild but very pleasant smoke, especially when I had it—in the morning with no breakfast. Past the half, I flicked the ash because I thought it was burning hotter through the middle and I was right. I touched it up with my torch and all was fine.

It went like this through to the end, with the flavors really not changing much and the burn being off and needing touch ups on several occasions. When the cigar was down to the last quarter I even put it down for a bit to cool off. I relit it and it tasted and burned fine, picking up a little strength but otherwise remaining the same. When it was down to the last inch, the flavors turned on me and I put it down.

I enjoyed it, and my Belgian friend who sent it to me posted a price of 8.90 Euros a stick in Europe. That's a very reasonable price for this cigar. I would buy these if they ever came my way. They're a very easy smoking cigar and as I said, a nice morning smoke. Thanks again, J.M.

—M.S.

Fonseca was a groundbreaker. He was famous for wrapping his cigars in fine Japanese tissue paper (as they still are today) and he was among the first to package cigars in metal tubes. Fonseca died in Havana of a heart attack in 1929. His wife Teresa continued to run the company until she eventually merged the brand with T. Castañeda and G. Montero, forming Castañeda, Montero, Fonseca SA.

Post revolution and today, Fonseca cigars continue to be a popular cigar brand around the world, but sales are strongest in Spain and Canada.

## CIGARS

- Cosacos
- Delicias
- KDT Cadetes

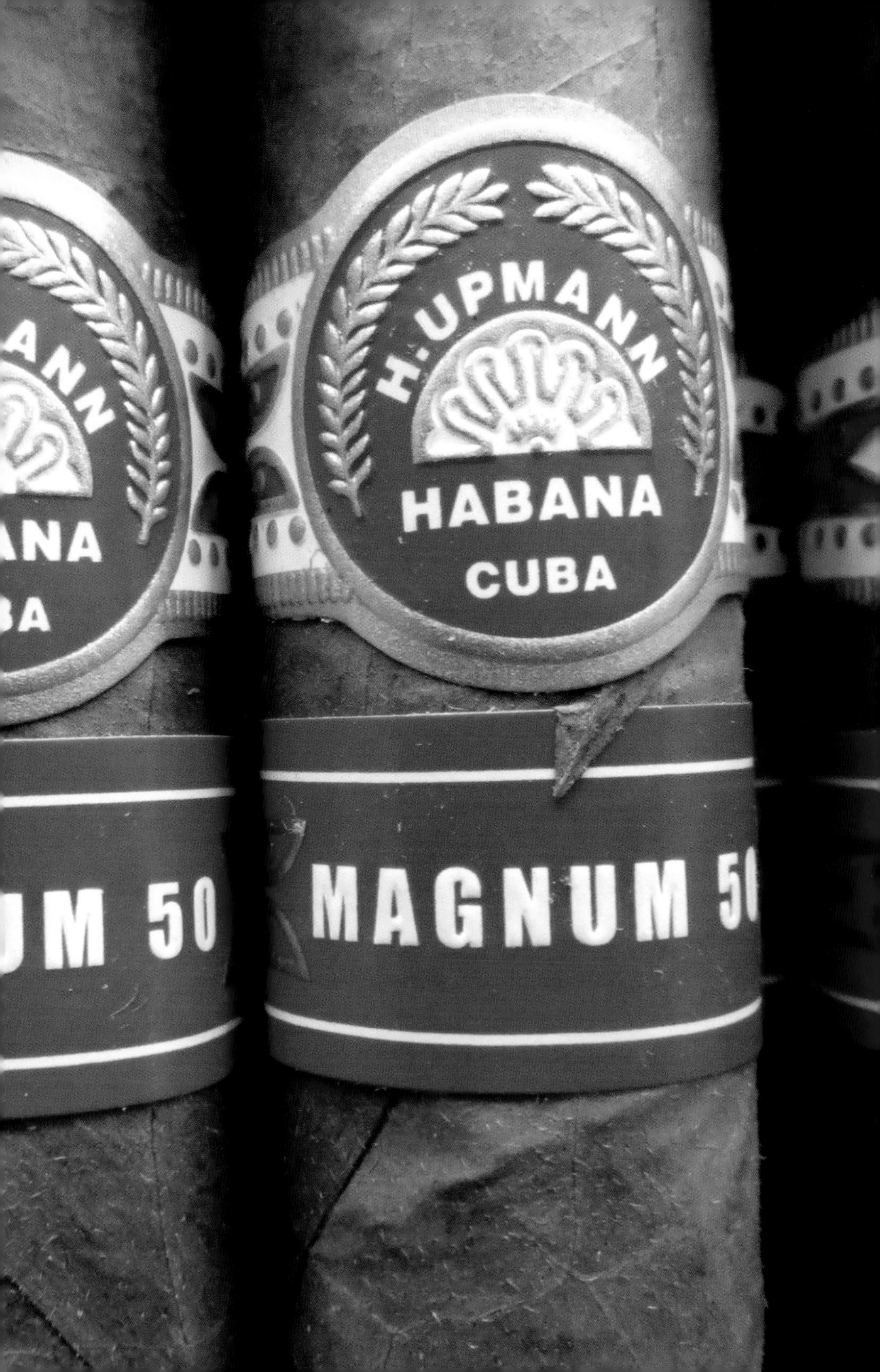
H. UPMANN
HABANA
CUBA
MAGNUM 50

# H. UPMANN

## STRENGTH: LIGHT TO MODERATE

H. Upmann is one of the oldest and most storied cigar brands in the world. The company dates back to 1844, when banker Herman Upmann (along with his brother August) first established a branch office in Havana. This gave H. Upmann the opportunity to ship cigars back to England and Europe. His shipments became so popular that he invested in a cigar factory in 1844, and the H. Upmann brand was established.

H. Upmann was among the first to package cigars in cedar boxes. Upmann used this as both a means of shipping as well as product introduction. The famous H. Upmann Factory is now known as the José Martí Factory, which is located in Havana.

Renowned for quality and craftsmanship, the H. Upmann brand won seven gold medals at various exhibitions over the last century. These have become part of the company's logo, which also features the founder's signature.

During hard economic times in the 1920s, the H. Upmann Bank and cigar business was sold to J. Frankau & Co. who purchased the brand and continued production and distribution. In 1935, H. Upmann changed hands again to newly established Menendez, García y Cía, which produced the Montecristo brand. Menendez, García y Cía continued production of H. Upmann up until the Cuban Revolution in 1959, after which the tobacco industry was nationalized.

Ironically enough, the Petit Upmann (now discontinued, sold under the name Demi Tasse in the United States) was allegedly the favorite cigar of United States President John F. Kennedy while he was in office and at diplomatic odds with Cuba. The night before Kennedy signed the Cuban embargo, he assigned Press Secretary Pierre Salinger to purchase every box he could find in the Washington, D.C., metro area. Salinger swooped up an impressive 1,200 cigars for the commander-in-chief.

The Cuban continues to be made in an original factory in Havana, and still uses tobacco from the highly acclaimed Vuelta Abajo region.

The H. Upmann Cuban-made cigars remain coveted on the international market. In 2002, Altadis SA purchased a controlling share in Habanos S.A. The line was revitalized and older styles were replaced by more popular ones. In 2005, Habanos S.A. unexpectedly began offering a new H. Upmann cigar as part of their annual Edición Limitada release.

## CIGARS

- Connoisseur No. 1
- Coronas Junior
- Coronas Major
- Coronas Minor
- Epicures
- Half Corona
- Magnum 46
- Magnum 50
- Majestic
- Petit Coronas
- Regalias
- Sir Winston
- Upmann No. 2

# ✬ H. UPMANN NO. 2 ✬

This has got to be one of my favorite Torpedoes, and I hadn't had one in years. I was given one by a friend who was at a Canada Day picnic in the park. It wasn't a particularly pretty cigar; a little bumpy, mottled, and covered in plume. I didn't care—looks can often be deceiving when it comes to cigars. The fact that it had seven years on it was all I could think about. The pre-light draw was all wood, I even got some splinters on my lips.

Once lit, the burn was good and the wood flavors really came through. But once I got past the first inch it was earthy and dry. The burn was a little off at a point and the cigar was the usual medium body, like I remembered. Past the first third it was unmistakably an Upmann No. 2: smooth, medium-bodied, with flavors of earth and wood. Past the half I found it burning hotter through the middle and then it went out. I had to relight it.

And so it continued like this until the end, with the flavors not changing much and burning pretty well until I decided to give it up. I enjoyed this cigar and appreciated the opportunity to give it a try after seven years of being packaged. It still had good taste and could probably lie down for a couple of more years before worrying about dissipating flavors.

—M.S.

# ★ H. UPMANN ROYAL ROBUSTO ★
## LA CASA DEL HABANO EXCLUSIVO 2011

I bought this box in Cuba in 2014 at the Club Havana La Casa del Habano (LCDH). There were several boxes, but this one was the only one with a 2012 box date. Someone had told me that anything from 2012 was smoking well and so I couldn't resist, and I'm glad I picked it up. To my understanding, these were released in 2011 and that only 5,000 dress boxes of ten cigars were made. This is a Robusto, weighing in at 52 x 135 (5.3").

This bumpy cigar with a bumpy cap was hard to the touch but veinless. I got little to nothing on the pre-light draw, but the draw itself was perfect. It started out mild with notes of wood and hints of nuts and earth. By the time I got to the first inch, the burn was a little off. This was definitely a mild cigar and after the first inch I touched it up with my torch.

I flicked the ash at about the quarter mark and the flavor remained unchanged. The burn was fine for about another quarter, but by the time I reached the half it was off again and so I touched it up again…and then again.

And so it went. The flavor didn't change, the burn was a bit uneven, the draw was bang on. This was a mild, uncomplicated cigar. Many people swear by it and I really enjoyed it. I think it may be a bit too mild for anyone who enjoys a full-bodied cigar, but I like many flavor profiles and strengths. For me, this is a go-to cigar, maybe a morning smoke or something to start a multi-cigar night.

I'm sorry I can't say more about this cigar but it really wasn't that complicated. However, I can tell you this: I put it down because I couldn't hold it any longer. If I can smoke a cigar down that far, anyone who knows me will tell you that's an endorsement.

—M.S.

# HOYO DE MONTERREY

## STRENGTH: MILD

In 1831, a 13-year-old Don José Gener y Batet made the long oversea journey from Spain to Cuba. Gener worked on his uncle's tobacco plantation in Vuelta Abajo, where he received an apprentice education. In 1865, he established his own cigar factory in Havana and began manufacturing La Escepción. The brand was popular, and he used the profits to purchase one of the highest quality tobacco farms in Vuelta Abajo. He called it Hoyo de Monterrey, "The hole of Monterrey," which referred to the bowl-shaped terrain prized by quality tobacco growers.

Hoyo de Monterrey became hugely popular in the British market and the factory subsequently became one of the largest in Cuba. In 1900, Gener died in Spain and his daughter, Lutgarda Gener, took over the family business. It would stay in the family for another thirty years.

The Gener family spun off their cigar unit in order to concentrate their efforts on their considerable sugar cane properties. In 1931, Fernández, Palicio y Cía purchased the Hoyo de Monterrey and La Escepción brands.

These two new properties fit perfectly with the firm's Punch and Belinda cigar lines. In 1958, Ramón Fernández died, leaving partner Fernando Palicio as the sole owner. That same year, the combined sales of Palicio's brand accounted for 13 percent of all Havana cigar exports.

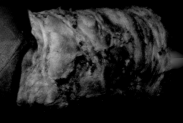

# ✴ HOYO DE MONTERREY PETIT ROBUSTOS ✴

I wasn't shopping for this cigar when I was visiting friends at different cigar shops in Havana, but when I found it, I couldn't resist picking it up. I'm pretty sure I smoked one a decade ago when it was first released in 2004, but I can't remember anything about the experience. I can tell you I like the size—50 x 102 (4.0")—it makes for a nice short smoke when you don't have the time for something bigger.

This particular cigar was hard as a rock but I've learned not to worry about that. Sure enough, the draw was perfect. It had a slightly bumpy cap with a veinless, light-colored wrapper. When first lit, it was almost a medium body with flavors of coffee and toasted nuts. It had an even burn, but by the time I got to the first inch it was slightly off and it mellowed out to become a mild smoke.

I touched it up with my torch past the first inch and the coffee and nuts made room for wood, which stayed right to the end. It wasn't a complicated cigar and it didn't change at all after that first inch. At the last third, it was burning a little hotter through the middle. I fixed it with my torch and it didn't affect the flavors at all. I smoked it right down to the end, and I have to say, I enjoyed it.

If you like a cigar with a bit of a kick, this one's not for you. If you like a little variety in your humidor and want a quick smoke with your morning coffee, this is a cigar to consider. I have no regrets buying this box, even though it isn't one of the most memorable cigars I'll smoke in my life.

—M.S.

After the Cuban revolution, Hoyo de Monterrey continued producing in Cuba (as well as in Honduras), and remains a popular global brand.

## CIGARS

- Coronations
- Double Coronas
- Epicure Especial
- Epicure No. 1
- Epicure No. 2
- Le Hoyo de San Juan
- Le Hoyo des Dieux
- Le Hoyo du Depute
- Le Hoyo du Gourmet
- Le Hoyo du Maire
- Le Hoyo du Prince
- Palmas Extra
- Petit Robustos

HOYO de MONTERREY
de
JOSÉ GENER
HABANA

MADE IN HAVANA, CUBA

ESTE PRODUCTO
PUEDE SER DAÑINO
PARA SU SALUD Y
CREA ADICCION.

MINSAP

Habanos D.O.P.

DENOMINACIÓN DE ORIGEN PROTEGIDA

HOYO de MONTERREY
de
JOSÉ GENER
HABANA

HABANA · CUBA

Habanos

DENOMINACIÓN DE ORIGEN PROTEGIDA

# JOSE L. PIEDRA

## STRENGTH: MODERATE TO FULL

Vicente and Jose Lamadrid created Jose L. Piedra in 1880. The tobacco is grown in the highly prized Vuelta Arriba region, while the cigars themselves are produced in Holguín, Cuba. Jose L. Piedra is a strong and popular brand in Cuba itself. The brand was temporarily discontinued in 1990, and then reinstated in 1996. Jose L. Piedra produces seven handmade cigars. It's a very competitively priced line for a well-made product.

## CIGARS

- Brevas
- Cazadores
- Conservas
- Cremas
- Nacionales
- Petit Cazadores
- Petit Cetros
- Royal Palms
- Superiores

# JUAN LOPEZ

**STRENGTH: MODERATE**

Spanish businessman Juan Lopez Diaz founded his namesake brand in 1876, in Havana, Cuba. The tobacco is procured from the famous Vuelta Abajo region and the cigars are produced in limited quantities. This is one of the few cigar brands whose entire lineup is handmade. It has a loyal and devoted following and is a favorite of aficionados.

## CIGARS

- Petit Coronas
- Selección No. 1
- Selección No. 2

# ✶ JUAN LOPEZ IDEALES EDICION ✶
# REGIONAL AUSTRIA 2011

A good friend of mine gave me this cute little box of cigars as a gift for my birthday when I was in Havana one time. What better place to smoke one (and I did), but I don't review cigars in Cuba. I smoked one after I got home and these are my thoughts.

The cigar weighed in at 50 x 102 (4") and is considered a Petit Robusto, a great size when you don't have a lot of time to smoke a cigar. They were released in 2011 in numbered slide boxes of ten cigars and 2,500 boxes were made.

The cigar was veinless and bumpy, with a little give when squeezed. The cap was a bit mushy. I got chocolate from the first draw, which seemed to be good. A little further into the cigar, I started picking up cedar flavors. By the time I got to about three-quarter-inch mark, the burn was off so I touched it up when I got to the first inch. The burn continued to be off throughout the cigar and I found myself continually touching it up.

Overall, it's a medium-bodied cigar that doesn't change much in flavor until the last third. At that point, it began to pick up strength and became earthy.

A very uncomplicated cigar, easy to smoke, and perfect for a short timeframe. Is it ready to smoke? I don't think time is going to make this cigar any better, but it may take a bit of the edge off the last third. I enjoyed this cigar and thank my friend Kolja for gifting them to me.

—M.S.

TABACOS

# LA FLOR DE CANO

**STRENGTH: MEDIUM**

La Flora de Cano was founded in 1884 by Tomas and Jose Cano. The tobacco is grown in the highly regarded Vuelta Abajo region, and the cigars are made in El Rey del Mundo. This is a small, mixed fill, mid-range cigar. The cigars are often hard to find due to small production quantities.

## CIGARS

- Petit Corona
- Selectos

# ✶ LA FLOR DE CANO GRAN CANO ✶
## EDICION REGIONAL GRAN BRETAÑA 2013

This was one of a few cigars that a friend of mine from Turkey sent me. He was on a trip to the U.K. and knew I wanted something from that region. This particular cigar didn't travel well; it had flattened out a bit and some of the wrapper was peeling off.

I have a tiny vial of liquid that I use to repair cigars called El Ligador and it has done a great job of repairing a few sticks of mine that have met the same fate. I did the touch-up a few weeks before and although I could make out a remaining crack or two, the liquid had done an excellent repair job. My only worry was that it might open up on me after it was lit. I can tell you now that this didn't happen and that I had no issues with this cigar, construction-wise, throughout the time I smoked it.

This cigar is known as a Gordito or a Robusto Extra and weighs in at 50 x 141 (5.6"). They were a 2013 release with an unknown amount of numbered boxes of ten cigars being produced.

This cigar had a bumpy cap—actually it was kind of bumpy all over, with a little give when squeezed. I tasted a bit of cedar on the pre-light draw. Once lit, I picked up big wood with earthy undertones and a hint of floral and citrus. The draw was perfect. That hint of floral and citrus disappeared almost immediately, making way for only the wood and earth, with leather coming into the picture when I neared the second half.

The burn was off right from the start and continued that way, to some degree or another, all the way through. I flicked the ash at the first inch and touched up the cigar with my torch.

The ash fell on its own past the halfway mark and what began as a slightly stronger than medium-bodied cigar turned out to be closer to mild. Very smooth for a cigar this young, I actually couldn't tell that this cigar was only a year old. The final half was all about leather and wood and I was able to smoke it down to the end with no unpleasant flavors creeping in. It did go out a couple of times and the burn was still off, but otherwise an excellent cigar.

I didn't find this cigar very complicated but I was very surprised at how smooth it was for such a young cigar. I don't know what a little time will do to it, but it smoked pretty well during the time I had it. If the price is right and if you're not into overly strong cigars I suggest trying this one if you can get your hands on it. It's also a good cigar for a novice cigar smoker.

—M.S.

# LA GLORIA CUBANA

**STRENGTH: MODERATE TO FULL**

In 1885, the Sociedad Cabañas y Castro established the La Gloria Cubana brand. The line of cigars was met with success and was sold to José F. Rocha in 1905. Rocha produced the brand in his factory at 364 Miguel Street in Havana for decades. In 1954, the Cifuentes family bought both La Gloria Cubana and Bolívar from Rocha's portfolio after his death. Manufacturing was then relocated to the Partagás factory (currently named the Francisco Pérez Germán factory). Though the brand disappeared briefly after the revolution, the Partagás factory relaunched the cigar in 1965. The La Gloria Cubana line is produced elsewhere today.

La Gloria Cubana also produces two machine-made cigarillos: the Mini and the Purito. La Gloria Cubanas are produced in small quantities, and the brand enjoys an excellent reputation with cigar lovers, with the Medaille d'Or No. 2 being a particularly prized cigar. It's among the most sought after of Cuban cigar exports.

## CIGARS

- Medaille d'Or No. 2
- Medaille d'Or No. 4

# ✶ LA GLORIA CUBANA BELUX NO.1 EDICION ✶
## REGIONAL BELUX 2011

This was a nice looking cigar sent to me by a friend of mine who lives in Belgium. The cigar was what's called the Genio size: 52 x 140mm (5.5"), a Robusto Extra. Belux stands for Belgium and Luxembourg, which means this cigar is only sold in those two countries. Only 3,500 boxes of ten were made.

The cigar was hard to the touch, with very little give. It had a bumpy cap and an almost dark, veinless, slightly bumpy, oily wrapper. The pre-light draw gave off notes of cedar. After lighting, the first draw had a good pull with earthy flavors. The burn was off just a little, but I touched it up anyway. I picked up lots of wood, even getting a few splinters on my lips. When I flicked the ash I noticed a nice cone, which meant the cigar was burning perfectly.

The flavors didn't change much and neither did the strength; it was a good, solid medium. At about a third to the end I picked up some slight floral notes, but that was only for a few minutes and then it was back to the strong wood.

I let it go out at about a quarter to the end and relit it after a few minutes. It was still smoking good with the same woody taste, no change. Shortly after, the cigar started to turn and I put it down.

This was a nice cigar and I really like this size. I think a couple of years will do it good but it's not smoking too badly now. I think some time might add a little complexity to this smoke. I have another one that I'm going to have to put away for a bit.

—M.S.

MONTECRISTO

HABANA · CUBA

OPEN

ESTE P
PUEDE S
PARA S
CREA A
M

# MONTECRISTO

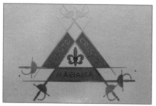

## STRENGTH: MODERATE TO FULL

Inspired by the classic novel by Alexandre Dumas, *The Count of Monte Cristo*, Alonso Menendez created this titular brand in July of 1935. Menendez bought the factory that made the beloved Particulares and the less-popular Byron brands, the Particulares. Legend has it that the Dumas book was a favorite among the *torcedores* (cigar rollers). In those days, a reader would read aloud to the rollers while they worked, and this particular title was the most popular. It is no surprise that the book's hero is a cigar smoking character named Edmond Dantés.

After purchasing the Particulares factory, Menedez immediately began to create the Montecristo brand. John Hunter Morris and Elkan Co. Ltd., the brand's British distributor, designed the now-famous Montecristo logo, which consists of a triangle of six swords surrounding a fleur-de-lis. The brand, and the logo, were an immediate hit.

A year after the purchase of the factory, Menendez established a new firm with his partner, naming it Menendez, García y Cía. With the profits from the wildly successful Montecristo brand, the firm bought the faltering H. Upmann factory in 1937. Production of Montecristo was transferred from the Particulares factory to the H. Upmann facility. This factory continued as the home of the Montecristo brand after the Cuban Revolution.

The original line of Montecristo had only five numbered sizes. A tubed cigar was added to the lineup sometime in the 1940s, which went undisturbed until after nationalization. With Menendez and García gone after

1959, when the brand was annexed by the government, one of the most accomplished of the *torcedores*, José Manuel Gonzalez, was promoted to manager and introduced new sizes and styles to the line. In the 1970s and 1980s Gonzalez added five new sizes.

## CIGARS

- Double Edmundo
- Eagle
- Edmundo
- Joyitas
- Junior
- Master
- Media Corona
- Montecristo A
- Montecristo Especial No. 2
- Montecristo No. 1
- Montecristo No. 2
- Montecristo No. 3
- Montecristo No. 4
- Montecristo No. 5
- Montecristo Tubos
- Petit Edmundo
- Petit No. 2
- Petit Tubos
- Regata

## ✶ ALFRED DUNHILL AND MONTECRISTO ✶

Born in 1872, Alfred Dunhill was an English tobacconist and inventor who established the Dunhill luxury goods company and Dunhill branded tobacco products.

In 1893, Alfred Dunhill established a company selling motoring accessories and by 1902 opened an exclusive shop in Mayfair. In 1904, he invented a pipe designed for motorists and he soon opened a tobacconist's shop in St. James's where he offered custom tobacco blends. During the 1920s, he added new stores in New York and Paris. As his brand began to increase in scope and value, he helped create the international modern luxury goods market.

Through the efforts of the Alfred Dunhill company, the Montecristo brand became immensely popular around the world. Dunhill sold the brand in his London shop, and promoted the brand heavily for its quality and uniqueness. Known for his excellent taste in promoting luxury goods, the Montecristo gained fame as being a fashionable cigar. Today, Montecristo accounts for approximately one quarter of Habanos S.A.'s worldwide cigar sales. The Montecristo is the most popular Cuban cigar in the world.

# ✦ MONTECRISTO NO. 1 CLUB HABANA ✦
## LA CASA DEL HABANO SPECIAL EDITION

On my trip to Cuba in August 2014, a friend made me aware of this special box while visiting the Club Havana La Casa del Habano (LCDH). His words were, "If you're going to buy anything, buy this." He thought of it as a collectible, but I thought of it as something to share with friends. The fifteen cigars inside were selected by the Partagás store and packaged with an additional band.

The cigars themselves, if you take them at their value, would cost you about $40 total but buying them this way means you're left with a lovely Partagás Book Humidor, which is small but worth the $162 CUC price tag.

As for the cigars themselves, I know nothing about them except that they had a few years of age on them. The store did a great job of selecting them because I've gone through six so far. I, along with the others who have shared their opinions with me, all agree that these are wonderful cigars.

From start to finish this was a Monte No. 1, mild, not near medium, smooth—I loved it. The burn was good until almost the end. The flavors were wood and wood with some earth creeping in, getting a bit more prominent closer to the end. The cigar was pretty much the same from the beginning and following through to almost the end. In the last quarter, the earthiness kicked it up a notch and the cigar got a little stronger.

This cigar was nothing special, that is to say it wasn't rolled specifically for this special box. However, all the cigars in the box have been wonderful smokes so far and well worth the money. Consistency is a beautiful thing, and if you can find that with Cuban cigars, even better. The Partagás store does it all the time, especially during the Encuentro.

—M.S.

# PARTAGÁS

**STRENGTH: FULL**

The Catalan Don Jaime Partagás y Ravelo was born in Arenys de Mar in 1816. He was the son of a tailor, Jaume Partagás, and his wife, Teresa Ravelo. Don Jaime immigrated to Cuba in 1831 where he worked for Joan Conill, a businessman in Lloret de Mar. In 1845, Don Jaime established his factory, La Flor de Tabacas de Partagás, at 1 Cristina Street in Havana.

Don Jaime owned and operated some of the best-quality tobacco producing plantations in the Vuelta Abajo region. He was able to choose the best of the best in making his blends, ensuring that his highest-quality cigars were always among the best made in Cuba. He was an innovator who experimented with numerous ideas regarding fermentation and tobacco aging. Don Jaime was also among the first and most celebrated owners for hiring readers to entertain the *trocedores* (cigar rollers) as they worked throughout the factory.

In 1868, his son Jose Partagás took over the business after his father was found murdered on one of the family's plantations.

Partagás changed hands several times after this, most notably in 1916, when it was purchased by Cifuentes, Pego y Cía. This firm became a powerhouse. It acquired such brands as Ramon Allones, the Bolívar and La Gloria Cubana brands, and also launched the Cifuentes brand. By 1958, Cifuentes was second only to the H. Upmann company in exporting Cuban cigars, controlling 25 percent of the export market.

FLOR DE TABACOS DE PARTAGAS Y CA. HABANA

FLOR DE TABACOS DE
PARTAGAS
Y CA.
HABANA

REPUBLICA DE CUBA

FLOR DE TABACOS

EXPOSITION UNIVERSELLE DE 1878.

LE JURY INTERNATIONAL DES RECOMPENSES

DECERNE

UN RAPPEL DE MÉDAILLE D'OR

À

Monsieur PARTAGAS

PARTAGAS
HABANA-CUBA

Partagás has enjoyed an immensely popular reputation, making it the second best selling brand of Cuban cigars after Montecristo. Partagás produces and distributes more than 10 million cigars annually.

The old Partagás Factory in Havana has been renamed Francisco Pérez Germán. It remains a well-visited tourist destination for cigar aficionados traveling in Cuba. Partagás manufacturing was moved in 2012.

# CIGARS

- Aristocrats
- Chicos
- Coronas Junior
- Coronas Senior
- Culebras
- de Luxe Tubos
- Habaneros
- Lusitanias

- Mille Fleurs
- Mini Collection 2012
- Petit Coronas Especiales
- Presidentes
- Salomones
- Serie D No. 4

- Serie D No. 5
- Serie D No. 6
- Serie E No. 2
- Serie P No. 2
- Shorts
- Super Partagás

# ★ PARTAGÁS SALOMONES ★

Monday night is usually smoke night for me, and on this occasion I was packed and ready to smoke something from my travel box but my host was kind enough to hand me a cigar upon my arrival at his place. He's quite the aficionado, with a walk-in humidor containing more stock than some of the stores I've entered in Toronto and certainly a stock of older stuff that's way better than any store in Cuba (except maybe the warehouse).

He doesn't even know what he has, and this was one of those times that he was moving some stuff around and found these two sticks in some corner of his humidor. Lucky for me, he was in a generous mood and I got to reminisce what the Partagás Salomones used to taste like. I don't have a box date for this cigar; they were not in any box when they were found. If I had to guess by its taste, I'd say this cigar was about seven to eight years old, around the time this cigar changed. It used to be a powerhouse of smoke with lots of flavor but for the last few years it's been toned down to something very mellow and easy to smoke. This is something that's been going on with just about all of the Partagás cigars, in my opinion.

The Salomon weighs in at 57 x 184 (7.2") and is known as a Double Perfecto. They have come in a dress box of ten cigars since 2008, and at some point have come with a La Casa del Habano band as well as the standard band (probably around the time of the change). The cigar I smoked only had the standard Partagás band, meaning that it was at least seven years old.

This cigar was as hard as a rock, I mean really hard. It would be a miracle if I could draw from this cigar. The slightly dark wrapper was a little bumpy and mottled. The pre-light draw was all wood. Once lit, the draw was a bit firm but smokable and I picked up bitter chocolate and burnt coffee bean flavors with a hint of wood…already completely different from a more current Salomon cigar. I couldn't tell which way the burn was going to go. From this beginning, I would say this was a medium-bodied cigar, venturing toward strong. These were the Salomones that I remembered from years ago.

Wood began to take over at the first inch and the burn was slightly off. The draw maintained its firmness. The burn was still slightly off passing the first inch but right after that it straightened itself out. I now tasted chocolate and wood and it was definitely between medium- to strong-bodied.

Past the second inch and the ash was still hanging on, until it finally fell on its own at about the two-and-a-half-inch mark. The burn was a little off, but I decide to leave it to see if it would fix itself again. Nearing the halfway mark this cigar was now overwhelmingly earthy with woody undertones. The burn certainly wasn't going to fix itself, so I touched it up with my torch. It got stronger. It seemed to be burning a bit hot due to the firmness and I had to hold back on the frequency of my draws even though I was afraid of it going out.

Into the third quarter of the cigar it was all earth; I couldn't taste anything else. It turned into a strong cigar that became a little difficult to smoke. It could have used a little more age (wow). Smoking the last quarter, the burn was way off. The cigar was going out and I had to do a touch-up and relight. The firmness added to the bitter taste near the end of this smoke and I finally had to give it up.

I was extremely happy to have been given the opportunity to try this cigar. It had been a long time since I'd had one of these (like this) and even when I did, so many years ago, it was only on a couple of occasions. In my opinion, the new Salomones don't hold a candle to the older ones. I believe that they've toned down this cigar and others to make them more appealing to the masses. However, the true aficionado is the one who suffers because of this marketing. If you can ever get ahold of a pre-2008 box of these, get it.

—M.S.

# ★ PARTAGÁS SELECCIÓN PRIVADA ★
## EDICIÓN LIMITADA 2014

I was lucky to have these gifted to me on my last trip to Cuba. This cigar is a Double Robusto and weighs in at 50 × 160 (6.3"). They will be packaged in dress boxes of ten cigars.

The cigars I was given had a darkish-colored wrapper that was smooth and oily but showing a few little bumps. The construction looked quite good. The pre-light draw tasted like chocolate but once lit it was all earth with a hint of roasted coffee bean. The draw was perfect and the burn pretty good nearing the first inch. At this point, it was a medium-body cigar. Past the first inch the burn was a bit off; still earth with a touch of wood.

A quarter way through the cigar and the burn was off enough for me to do a touch-up with my torch. It was all earth and continued to be medium body. And so it went to about the last quarter. I had to keep touching it up; it went out several times and I had to relight it. At one point I noticed it was burning hotter through the middle. None of this affected the taste of the cigar. It became a little stronger through the last quarter and finally it became too small for my taste to relight it again, so I let it go.

This cigar needs time to rest, but I was actually surprised by how well it smokes now. It reminds me of the Montecristo 520 and the Cohiba 1966, but without that in-your-face power. This one is definitely toned down in comparison to those two, but similar in flavor. It's very unlike the usual Partagás profile. I liked it, and I'm going to buy a box or two for putting aside. I recommend trying this cigar.

—M.S.

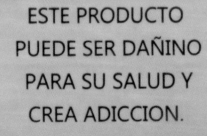

ESTE PRODUCTO
PUEDE SER DAÑINO
PARA SU SALUD Y
CREA ADICCION.

# POR LARRAÑAGA

## STRENGTH: LIGHT TO MODERATE

Ignacio Larrañaga established Por Larrañaga in 1834. Por Larrañaga had become a popular quality cigar brand by the late 1800s, manufacturing a portfolio of both high-end and inexpensive cigars. In 1925, Por Larrañaga was the first factory to make machine-made cigars, which upset many. Sales remained brisk for many decades, and Por Larrañaga was the sixth largest producing Cuban brand at the time of the revolution and beyond.

A well-known and respected brand up until the 1970s, the premium cigar brand soon experienced some changes. By the 1980s production had fallen off dramatically and further legal litigation reduced the territories for distribution. At its lowest point, Por Larrañaga produced mostly machine-made or hand-finished cigars, which were distributed in Canada and the Middle East. With new handmade versions, the brand has experienced a resurgence, in both image and quality, with all four vitolas being completely handmade.

Habanos S.A. produced some thousand boxes of Lonsdales, a discontinued favorite of Por Larrañaga aficionados, in 2006 for exclusive release in Germany. Twenty-five vitolas were presented in dress boxes and bore a special second band, reading "Exclusivo Alemania" (Germany Exclusive).

Today, Por Larrañga has been completely rebranded. Por Larrañga produces light to medium strength cigars, using tobacco from the premium Vuelta Abajo region. The current line-up of Por Larrañaga remains completely handmade. It is a small production house, and is highly sought prize among current Cuban cigar enthusiasts.

## CIGARS

- Montecarlos
- Panetelas
- Petit Coronas
- Picadores

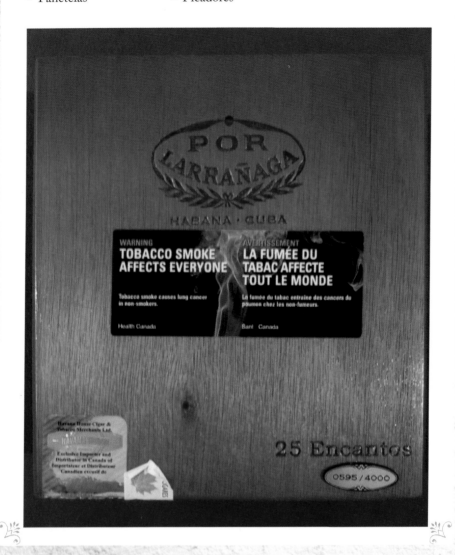

POR
LARRANAGA

HABANA

# ✶ POR LARRAÑAGA LONSDALE EDICION ✶ REGIONAL ALEMANIA 2006

This cigar was given to me a few weeks ago along with a few other beauties by a friend of mine from the U.S., of all places. He didn't know it at the time but I loved this cigar. I had the opportunity to smoke two of these not long after their release. The details are sketchy after all this time but I do remember how smooth and ready to smoke they were at such a short time after their release. They made 2,400 boxes of 25 of these Lonsdales (at 42 x 6½") and released them in 2006.

This box-pressed cigar was very solid to the touch, hard as a rock, and it had me worried. It had a bumpy cap and was kind of bumpy all over actually, with no really big veins just some small ones. The caramel colored wrapper was slightly mottled but it didn't look too bad and besides...it doesn't have an affect on the smoke. The pre-light draw was sweet, hints of ginger and confirmed that it was a tad tight.

Once lit, the draw had a bit of resistance but it was smokeable. This cigar was just as I remembered, smooth and mild. I tasted chocolate now, it was so creamy, and it reminded me of a Cohiba Lancero. At about the first eighth, I picked up hints of roasted hazelnut. A little while after that, a touch of wood. At the first quarter, the ash fell on its own and the burn was dead on. The flavors hadn't changed through the last eighth.

By the time I reached the halfway mark I began to taste a little more wood. When passing the half, the ash fell on its own again and the burn was just slightly off. I was beginning to taste a little bitterness now and again. The burn straightened itself out and it was beginning to pick-up strength nearing the last quarter. Just past the last quarter and the draw was just too tight to make this a pleasurable smoke at this point so I gave it up.

This was a very uncomplicated smoke. Mild and smooth. I remember a friend telling me a few years ago that he didn't like this smoke because it wasn't very exciting. He prefers a stronger smoke. I, on the other hand, like them all, mild and strong and everything in between. I enjoyed this cigar when I first smoked it several years ago and I still like it now. I believe they won't get better. The one I smoked, I'm sure, I would have been able to smoke right down to the end if it wasn't so tight. I'm thankful to have been able to smoke it to where I did and that what I did smoke wasn't affected by the firmness.

—M.S.

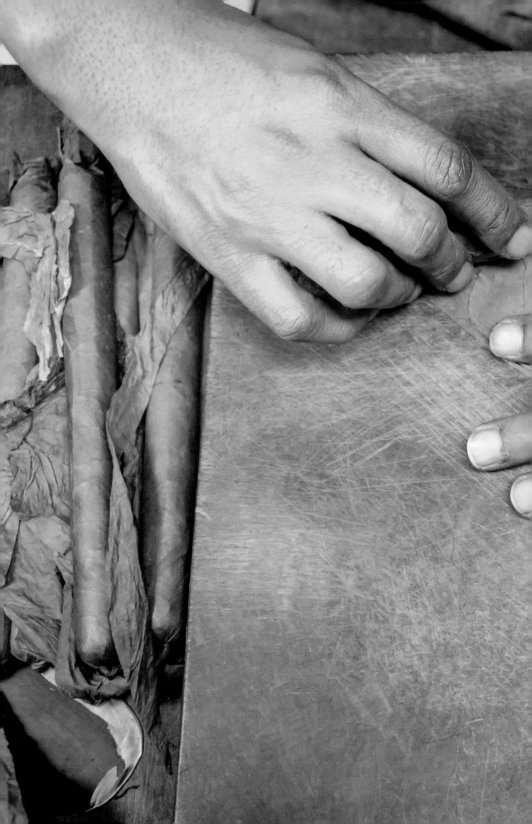

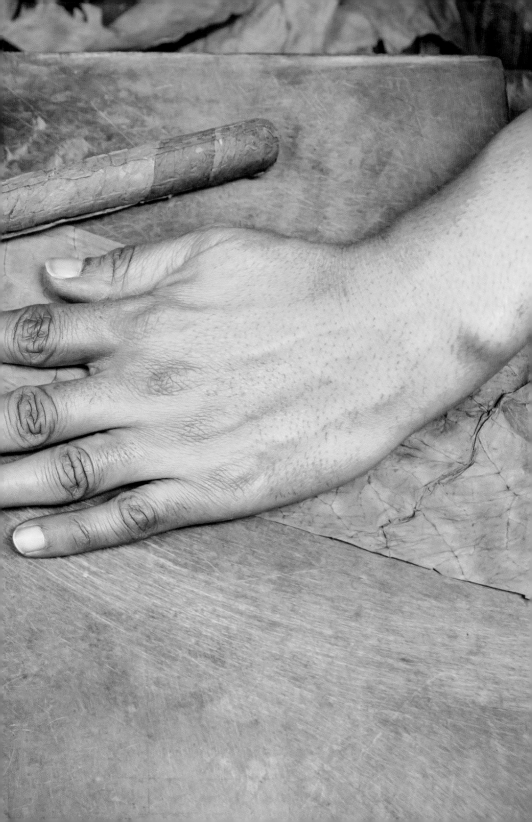

# PUNCH

**STRENGTH: FULL**

The Punch cigar was launched in 1840, and became a highly successful cigar in Victorian Britain. The brand was established by a German man named Stockman who had named the brand after the popular puppet show character, Mr. Punch of "Punch and Judy" fame. In 1874 the brand was purchased by Luis Corujo, and sold a decade later to Manuel López Fernández, whose name is still represented on the company's cigar bands and boxes. Fernandez

### ✶ MR. PUNCH ✶

Mr. Punch is a character from the Italian Comedia D'ella Arte that became a popular British children's character in Victorian Britain. Punch and Judy is a puppet show featuring Mr. Punch and his wife, Judy. The performance consists of a sequence of short scenes, each depicting an interaction between two characters, most typically Mr. Punch and one other character (who usually falls victim to the wrath of Mr. Punch's menacing club). These performances are often associated with traditional British seaside culture. The various episodes of Punch and Judy are performed in the spirit of outrageous comedy, and are dominated by the anarchic clowning of Mr. Punch.

ESTE PRODUCTO
PUEDE SER DAÑINO
PARA SU SALUD Y
CREA ADICCION.

MINSAP

MANUEL LOPEZ

retired in 1924, and the brand suffered severe economic hardship under the ownership of Esperanza Valle Comas, who oversaw it for only a few years before the stock market crash of 1929.

While still maintaining popularity in the UK, the firm Fernández, Palicio y Cía purchased Punch in 1930. Punch then grew with the favorites, Belinda, La Escepción, and Hoyo de Monterrey, and became one of the company's lead cigar marques.

Punch continued production in post-revolutionary Cuba. Among cigar aficionados, the eponymous Punch, Double Corona, Churchill, and Super Selection No. 2 are especially prized and sought after.

## CIGARS

- Coronations
- Double Coronas
- Petit Coronations
- Punch-Punch
- Royal Coronations

# ✷ PUNCH DOUBLE CORONA ✷

The cigar came from a 50 cabinet box, marked 2002–03, and like every Cuban Double Corona it weighed in at 49 x 194 (7.6") and it was a beautiful specimen. A friend shared his stash with me.

This Double Corona, with its dark caffè latte colored wrapper was as hard as a rock and on the pre-light draw it was all wood. It was slightly oily and a little bumpy but had no visible veins. Once lit, I tasted earth and wood; not complicated at all. The burn started a bit off but upon nearing the first inch it straightened itself out. Passing the first inch the wood was replaced by grass and, it may have been my taste buds, but it seemed a little dry. This was a medium to strong bodied cigar at this point. Past around the 2-inch mark the ash fell on it's own leaving a nice little cone, the sign of a well-rolled cigar. The edge was coming off this cigar and the flavor was closer to a medium body and distinct earthiness.

At around the halfway mark the ash fell on its own again, this time it was burning a little hotter through the middle...nothing terribly serious but I touched it up just the same. I was enjoying this cigar so much I didn't want anything to disrupt that pleasure. It went out nearing the last third, but that may have been due more to my own distraction, rather than a poorly rolled cigar. The strength picked up at this point, becoming medium to strong again with a rally towards the strong side at the last quarter. I can assure you that I smoked this sucker right down to the end with no problem, it didn't turn on me.

In conclusion, wow, just wow. This is what a Punch DC should taste like. I've had a few boxes in my time but nothing older than a 2009 and what I smoked, even though they were nice cigars, were quite mild. I thank my friend for having me over and sharing this wonderful cigar with me.

—M.S.

# QUAI D'ORSAY

## STRENGTH: LIGHT

The Quai d'Orsay line of cigars was established by Cubatabaco in 1973, and intended for the French state tobacco monopoly, SEITA (La Societe Nationale d'Exploitation Industriel de Tabac et Allumettes). The profile of this brand was a handmade cigar that was light to moderate in flavor, and made specifically to appeal to French tastes. The brand's name is a reference to the Parisian avenue of the famous Left Bank of the Seine River, which runs through the heart of Paris. It is also no coincidence that the French Foreign Ministry, the same location where SEITA headquarters was located, was on Quai d'Orsay Avenue.

The cigar's range is made of light (Claro) to mid-brown (Colorado Claro) wrappers, which is to French tastes, and the flavor is smooth and light, also to French tastes. The tobacco for the cigars comes from the Vuelta Abajo region, and the cigars are made at the Romeo y Julieta factory.

## CIGARS

- Coronas
- Imperiales

# ★ QUAI D'ORSAY BELICOSO ROYAL EDICION ★
# REGIONAL FRANCIA 2013

I traded for a couple of these cigars with a friend of mine who lives in France. Two thousand numbered boxes of 25 cigars were released in January 2014. It weighed in at 52 x 125 (4.9"), a Petit Belicoso. The light-colored wrapper on this one was smooth and oily, and was flawless. It was hard to the touch with just a hint of give. The pre-light draw gave me dried fig and wood and it seemed like the draw was going to be a bit firm. Once lit, my suspicions were confirmed, it was a bit tight. I opted to cut a little more off. That seemed to make it a little better. The burn was way off right from the start so I touched it up. A half inch into this cigar and I tasted a sweetness, chocolate, with wood and a hint of floral. The burn continued to be off, this was a medium to strong bodied cigar.

I left the cigar for a moment at about the first inch mark and it went out. The burn was still off. It was still a bit stronger than a medium body, a nice full-bodied medium. Into the second quarter of this cigar and I picked up leather and wood. The burn was still off. The draw turned out to be okay, just a little firm.

Near the halfway mark and the burn was way off again and burning hotter through the middle. I had to do a major touch-up. It was starting to turn on me already, very earthy at this point and that hint of floral came in for a moment. Into the third quarter of the cigar and leather was the dominant flavor, with that hint of floral coming around for a moment once again. The last quarter was earthy and it went out again...I didn't bother re-lighting.

This cigar was all over the place and took a bit of work to smoke with all the re-lights and touch-ups but I enjoyed it just the same. It definitely was a very interesting smoke and very young, it likely needs a couple of years to rest. I have one more and will put it away for a much later date. If you decide to buy a box I recommend that you stick it in the back of your humidor and try to resist temptation. This will be a much better cigar down the road.

—M.S.

# QUINTERO

## STRENGTH: MEDIUM

Quintero y Hermanos, or Quintero and Brothers as it is known now and in the English speaking world, was founded in 1924 by Agustin Quintero and his four brothers.

The Quintero's blend of tobacco was an immediate commercial success for the brothers, both in Cuba and abroad. The Quintero tobacco blend is unusual in that it holds a unique herbal flavor with sweet aftertaste. The cigars tend to ripen after several months of additional aging before being marketed. Originally, all the cigars were handmade.

The Quinteros brothers founded a small cigar factory in the town of Cienfuegos, Cuba. Cienfuegos, a city on the southern coast of Cuba, is near the tobacco growing region of Vuelta Arriba of the Remedios. Quintero is one of a small handful of Cuban cigar brands not originated in the prime tobacco growing region of Vuelta Abajo.

Quintero y Hermanos, as it was still known then, grew larger in the 1940s and moved to a much larger factory in Havana. They then began using high-quality tobaccos from the Vuelta Abajo growing region. The brand grew steadily. Sales increased domestically and worldwide and were particularly popular in Spain.

After the Cuban cigar industry was nationalized, the Quintero brand was repositioned. The company, now part of the national system, stopped making handmade cigars, and made machine-made cigars instead, or hand-finished cigars. Some of their cigars were sold in aluminum tubes or *tubos*. In the later part of the 20th century, Quintero and Brothers was the only Cuban machine-made brand to be sold globally, and their popularity in Spain never wavered.

In 2002, the Cuban government marketing organization, Habanos S.A., chose to reposition the brand once again. They discontinued selling machine-made cigars under the Quintero and Brothers label, and returned to making only handmade cigars. The Quintero cigar now markets itself as being *totalmente a mano* (totally handmade). Its cigars come in four sizes. These high quality, premium cigars are medium to full bodied in strength and are handmade with a short and medium filler blend of tobacco leaves from the Vuelta Abajo and Semi-Vuelta zones of the Pinar del Río region of Cuba.

## CIGARS

- Brevas
- Favoritos
- Londres Extra
- Nacionales
- Panetelas
- Petit Quinteros

# RAFAEL GONZALEZ

**STRENGTH:**

Previously known as La Flor de Marquez, this cigar was one of the most wildly successful cigars of the 1920s and 1930s. The brand dates back to 1928 (though it was not registered until 1936 by the Sociedad El Rey del Mundo) and the trademark records show that the name was changed to Rafael Gonzalez in 1945.

It has been speculated that it was La Flor de Marquez line that first introduced the Lonsdale size, named in honor of Hugh Cecil Lowther, the Fifth Earl of Lonsdale.

The tobacco is procured from the Vuelta Abajo tobacco growing region. The cigars are hand rolled, of medium body, and are considered by many to be a very high quality cigar.

## CIGARS

- Panetelas Extra
- Perlas
- Petit Coronas

# ✶ RAFAEL GONZALEZ PETIT PIRAMIDES ✶
## EDICION REGIONAL ALEMANIA 2013

I had read somewhere that this cigar was pretty mild, which isn't a negative in my book. It was sent to me by a friend who lives in Germany. Six thousand numbered dress boxes of 10 cigars were made in 2013 with an early 2014 release. The vitola is a Petit Pyramid and weighs in at 50 x 127 (5"), a nice, short smoke.

It was a decent looking cigar that appeared to be constructed well. It was hard to the touch, a little bumpy but veinless. I got nothing on the pre-light draw but got earthy flavors once lit. A little leather creeping in after the first half inch. This was definitely a mild cigar. It had a good draw but the burn was a little uneven. I eventually touched it up with my torch so it wouldn't get away from me. Passing the first inch, the flavors hadn't changed and it's still a mild smoke. I flicked the ash at about the one-and-a-half-inch mark. I was left with a nice cone shaped ash, a sign of a good roll.

Past the halfway mark I flicked the ash again, which was burning evenly at this point. The flavors still hadn't changed. It began to pick up strength with about an inch-and-a-half to go. Touched it up near the end, I couldn't hold it any longer.

Not a spectacular cigar but a very pleasant smoke nonetheless. I couldn't hold it anymore, that says it all. This cigar is a perfect morning smoke with a cup of coffee or a good starter cigar on those occasions when I smoke four to five in one sitting. In my opinion, worth the money, actually. I must add some to my collection. I liked it but don't expect big things from this cigar.

—M.S.

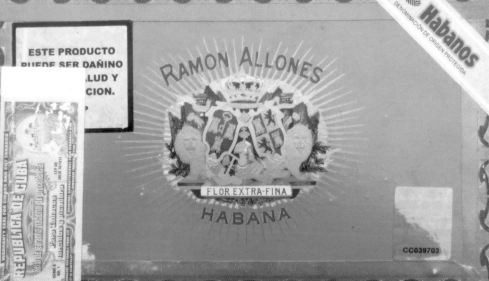

# RAMÓN ALLONES

## STRENGTH: FULL

Ranking amongst the oldest brands still in production, Ramón Allones was created in Cuba by Spanish immigrant brothers Ramón and Antonio Allones in 1837, and then officially established in 1845. Brothers Ramón and Antonio were exceptional marketers, and their ideas still influence cigar packaging to this day. Ramón Allones is credited, with some lasting dispute, as the first line of cigars to use colorful lithographs for box art. They are also credited with being the first to label each cigar individually with a band, and to package cigars in the "8-9-8" size and style. These two moves made them marketing pioneers in the field.

Like many of the other older Cuban cigar companies, the brand changed ownership many times over the next century. The company was purchased by the Cifuentes family, and then eventually Ramón Allones production was later moved to another facility. The entire line of these robust cigars is comprised of quality hand-rolled cigars. The blend created by its founders remains unchanged and widely appreciated.

The Ramón Allones line of cigars has remained highly-prized by aficionados through the decades.

## CIGARS

- Gigantes

- Small Club Coronas

- Specially Selected

# ⋇ RAMON ALLONES SUPERIORES ⋇
## LCDH EXCLUSIVO 2010

This cigar was originally released in 2010, 5,000 boxes of 10 cigars each were produced., I'm assuming this was a re-release because this box was dated April 2013. The cigar is considered a Corona Gorda and weighs in at 46 x 143 (5.6").

I bought this box in Havana about a year ago. I've smoked a couple in the past and remembered them being pretty good, so when I saw a 2013 box, at that price, I snatched it up.

The one I picked out of the box to smoke was as hard as a rock but had a perfect draw after all. The first half-inch gave me an even burn with flavors of chocolate and earth, it was mild to medium in strength. Once I reached the first inch it was becoming more earthy and was getting a little bitter. A little more into the smoke and it was increasingly earthy with grass. The bitterness had left at this point and it picked up a bit of strength. The burn was absolutely perfect and I flicked the ash around the half way mark...smoking indoors, I didn't want to make a mess.

Past the half the cigar started to mellow out again. In general it wasn't even remotely strong at any time. The burn went slightly off and with a third of the smoke remaining it picked up strength again. Smoked it to near the end.

A gem of a cigar that could use a little time in the humidor. It cost me 57.50 CUC in Cuba, how could I go wrong? Now I have to resist smoking them all before their time. If you see any when you're in Cuba, pick them up, definitely a good buy.

—M.S.

# ROMEO Y JULIETA

**STRENGTH: MEDIUM**

The Romeo y Julieta brand, established by Inocencio Alvarez and Manin Garcia in 1875, honors the famed tragedy of Shakespeare's star-crossed lovers.

Romeo y Julieta won several awards and medals between 1885 and 1900, which are prominently displayed on their logo. However, the cigar line experienced an even bigger explosion in popularity after it was purchased by Jose "Pepin" Rodríguez Fernandez and his company, Rodríguez, Argüelles y Cia, in 1903. Pepin, who had previously headed up the Cabañas factory in Havana, was a well-traveled gentleman who spent his time traveling between Europe and the Americas. He was aggressive in promoting his brand, and owned a famous horse, appropriately named Julieta, which he entered in races around the world. He used the success of his horse to promote his line quite often and effectively.

Sir Winston Churchill, prime minister of the United Kingdom, was perhaps the brand's most well-known fan. Romeo y Julieta's flagship vitola is named in Churchill's honor, a long 7" by 47-ring gauge cigar known as the Churchill. The shape and size are now a standard industry offering.

In 1954, at the ripe old age of 88, Pepin died, just 5 years before the Revolution. Still produced in Cuba, the brand is known worldwide as one of the country's top selling cigars.

- Belicosos
- Belvederes
- Cazadores
- Cedros De Luxe No. 1
- Cedros De Luxe No. 2
- Cedros De Luxe No. 3
- Churchills
- Coronitas en Cedro
- Exhibición No. 3
- Exhibición No. 4
- Julieta
- Mille Fleurs
- Petit Churchills
- Petit Coronas
- Petit Julieta
- Puritos
- Regalias De Londres
- Romeo No.1 Tubos
- Romeo No.2 Tubos
- Romeo No.3 Tubos
- Short Churchills
- Sports Largos
- Wide Churchills

# ✶ ROMEO Y JULIETA SHORT CHURCHILL ✶

This cigar was given to me about a year ago at a function. Believe it or not, I don't remember ever smoking one before now. This particular one was the bomb and well worth the wait. The box date was from 2012 and I had been saying for well over a year now that it was an excellent year for cigars in Cuba, in my humble opinion. It's considered a Robusto, weighing in at 50 x 124 (4.9") and has been sold in dress boxes of 10 and 25 cigars plus cardboard packs of 3 cigars in aluminium tubes since 2006.

The cigar was slightly bumpy but otherwise smooth. What scared me was that it was as hard as a rock and might prove to be too tight but the pre-light draw showed me otherwise. The draw was good. I picked up nothing at this point except for a little wood. Once lit, it was a mild to medium-bodied smoke with a woody flavor. For the first half-inch the burn was straight but after that and for almost the entire smoke the burn was off and I was constantly touching it up with my torch. I know many of my readers don't like it when I do that but I believe if you let the burn get away from you and canoe too much, it will alter the taste of the smoke.

By the first inch, the cigar was very smooth and had no rough edges, with hints of cocoa bean creeping in but still overwhelmingly woody. Not far past the first inch the ash fell on its own. The cigar was turning out to be more on the mild side. The flavors pretty much remain the same but just past the halfway mark some earthiness started to muscle its way in for a while and then began to take over past the remaining third of the cigar, making it the dominant flavor until the end. The entire time I was touching up the cigar with my torch to make sure the burn was relatively straight. By the last inch, it picked up strength but it still smoked well right to the very end.

Except for the burn being off, this was a flawless cigar. I enjoyed smoking this cigar immensely and would recommend the Short Churchill to any newbie smoker—it may be a little too mild for the seasoned enthusiast. This of course comes as no surprise since it's well known that Romeo y Julieta is one of the milder brands in the Cuban cigar catalog and this vitola is no exception. If you're a novice cigar smoker or an experienced aficionado looking for a breakfast smoke, this cigar is for you.

—M.S.

CHURCHILL

# ★ WINSTON CHURCHILL ★

One of the greatest wartime leaders of the 20th century, Sir Winston Leonard Spencer-Churchill (November 20, 1874 to January 24, 1965) was truly a renaissance man. Associated as a historian, a writer, and an artist; he was an officer in the British Army, received the Nobel Prize in Literature, and was prime minister of the United Kingdom during the war time years. He held this office from 1940 to 1945, and again from 1951 to 1955.

He was also a lover of cigars.

Churchill went to Cuba in 1895 searching for action and military glory by which he could distinguish himself. Cuba at the time was rebelling against Spain. It was in Cuba, Churchill wrote later, "where real things were going on. Here was a scene of vital action. Here was a place where anything might happen. Here was a place where something would certainly happen. Here I might leave my bones."

Staying in a grand hotel with little money, in November 1895, Churchill and a fellow officer lived on oranges and cigars. It was here that Churchill fell in love with the art of Cuban tobacco. Later in life he was known to smoke as many as fourteen cigars a day, many he left smoldering in ashtrays, happy to pick them up and chew on their smoky ends. At Chartwell Manor, his country estate in Kent, Churchill stored as many as 3,000–4,000 cigars at any time. Most of them were Cuban.

Later in life, after the Second World War, in 1946 Winston Churchill visited Havana. He made a special visit to Romeo y Julieta and met Simon Camacho (who later started his own brand in the United States). A special band was created to commemorate his tour of Cuba. Churchill's favorite size and gauge were named in his honor, and the Churchill cigar remains to this day one of the most popular sizes and styles.

# SAINT LUIS REY

**STRENGTH: FULL**

Saint Luis Rey brand was created in 1938 and the company established in 1940. The origins of this cigar's name are not known. Most likely, it was named for the town of San Luis in the Vuelta Abajo tobacco region of Cuba. This is where the cigars were originally produced. It has also been speculated that that they were named after the famous Thornton Wilder 1927 novel, *The Bridge of San Luis Rey*.

Today, these Cuban cigars are exclusively hand-rolled from tobacco grown in the Vuelta Abajo region. They are considered very, very good quality, competitively priced, and an excellent value.

## CIGARS

- Double Coronas
- Regios
- Série A

FABRICA DE TABACOS
SAINT LUIS REY

# SANCHO PANZA

**STRENGTH: MODERATE**

Established in 1852 by Emilio Ahmsted, this line of cigars was named for the rustic sidekick Sancho Panza, who rode alongside Don Quixote in the famed 1605 novel of the same name by the Spanish author Miguel de Cervantes.

Sancho Panza is a farmer, and recruited as a squire to serve Don Quixote in Cervantes' novel. Throughout the novel, Sancho provides earthly wisdom in the form of Spanish proverbs, and their subtle wisdom often surprise his master, Don Quixote. These bits of wisdom came to be known as sanchismos.

This mellow tasting, medium-bodied brand is much admired for its larger sizes, especially the gigantic Sanchos. The cigars are rolled at Romeo y Juilieta and the tobacco is grown in the famed Vuelta Abajo region.

## CIGARS

- Belicosos

- Non Plus

# ✭ SANCHO PANZA BELICOSO ✭

I had been wanting to buy a box of these cigars for years. This was one of the first boxes of cigars I bought on my very first trip to Cuba many years ago. I loved them then but haven't had one since, it's not a cigar most people have or that you'll find selling in singles. However, on my last trip to Havana I had put it in my head that not only was I going to pick up a box, I was going to look for something with a little age. My first and only stop was the Club Havana LCDH in Miramar that was not far from where I was staying. This cigar shop is known for having some gems in the way of Limited Editions and aged stuff.

I wasn't wrong, they had three boxes of the Sanchos that were from last year and this one that I purchased. It had been opened, several times, but nobody wanted them and I wondered why. Looking at them, they weren't too pretty and I imagined that may have been a turn off. The cigars were covered with a dusting of plume, the foot looked moldy and it smelled as such. I took a gamble thinking a store as prestigious as this one would not be selling a bad box of cigars. I was being taken care of by Jorge, the shop's master roller.

As I mentioned above, this wasn't a pretty cigar and the cap was no better. It was dry and hard to the touch but almost veinless. The pre-light draw gave me hints of earth, wood, and tea and left a peppery taste on my lips. As soon as I lit this cigar I got a whiff of caramelized sugar and the pepper left my mouth. After a few puffs, the cigar settled down and I got solid flavors of tea and wood. This was starting out as a big and strong cigar, it was very much as I remembered it, taste wise. Past the first half inch, the edge came off and it began to mellow out. Earthy was the dominant flavor at this point, with wood in the background. Passing the first inch it continued to get milder...another half inch and the burn was perfect...flavor unchanged.

Just before the halfway mark I flicked the ash. I had a feeling that the cigar was being stifled by the ash and I was correct, it was burning a little hot through the middle. The burn was still bang-on but the flavors still hadn't changed. It picked up a bit of strength through the last quarter and then eventually got a little too bitter for my taste.

I enjoyed this cigar and I'm happy I bought the box. It wasn't very complicated nor was it strong. It started out with a bang but quickly settled down to become a relatively mild cigar. I don't know if any more age will make them any better but it is unlike any of the other Piramides I've smoked...the Monte #2 might come close. Will smoke another one soon so I can compare.

—M.S.

# SAN CRISTOBAL
# DE LA HABANA

**STRENGTH: LIGHT TO MODERATE**

The name San Cristobal is possibly a nod to the Italian explorer who sailed under the Spanish flag, Christopher Columbus. However, the root for San Cristobal, which is now Havana, was the original name for Cuba's capital city founded in 1519 and named for the patron saint of the city, Saint Christopher, the protector of all travelers.

Another brand by the name of San Cristobal de la Habana existed in Cuba before the Revolution, but this newer lineup of premium cigar is completely unrelated and not a recasting of the old brand.

This line of San Cristobal de la Habana officially launched in Havana on November 20, 1999. The brand initially launched with four cigars, and five years later they added three new styles.

## CIGARS

- El Morro
- El Príncipe
- La Fuerza
- La Punta

# SAN CRISTOBAL DE LA HABANA

STE PRODUCTO
EDE SER DAÑINO
RA SU SALUD Y
REA ADICCION.

**MINSAP**

Habana

DENOMINACION DE ORIGEN PROTE

*La Habana-Cuba*

AC358088

# TRINIDAD

**STRENGTH: MODERATE**

Trinidad cigars for a long period of time were playfully considered a sort of "unicorn brand," something aficionados talked about frequently, but were rarely ever seen. From 1908 onward, Trinidad cigars were used largely as gifts by the Cuban government to foreign diplomats, which considering their lack of domestic distribution, only increased their legend.

The Trinidad line gained attention in the early 1990s, when the cigar received much attention in a *Cigar Aficionado* interview with Avelino Lara (former manager of El Laguito, a cigar producer). Though Lara claimed Fidel Castro was a fan, Castro in his autobiography claimed to know very little about the brand himself.

The tobacco comes from the famed Vuelta Abajo region. Trinidad cigars are made with a very similar tobacco blend as Cohiba, but doesn't receive the third barrel fermentation that is a signature of the Cohiba brand.

According to Cuban Cigar expert Adriano Martínez, a former executive of Habanos S.A., the Trinidad brand was first produced in 1969 at the El Laguito factory in Havana, where Cohibas are made.

In February 1998, the Trinidad brand was released for public consumption at an opening ceremony in the Habana Libre Hotel in Havana. The initial release featured only one size, the Fundador, which offered a nutty, rich, medium flavored smoke. Other sizes were subsequently added in later years. The cigars were first made available in Canada and Mexico in April 1998.

The cigar was named for the city of Trinidad, Cuba.

## CIGARS

- Coloniales
- Fundadores
- Reyes
- Vigia

# ✦ TRINIDAD VIGIA ✦

This cigar was gifted to me at the same time as some Cohiba Robusto Supremos, and I smoked the Trinidad right after the Cohiba. To say that it was a great cigar smoking day is an understatement. These two cigars were on the top of my list of "must try" and will now move to the list of "must buy" when they're finally released. Another magnificently rolled cigar, hard as a rock with a beautiful light colored wrapper and a perfect pigtail topping the cap. It was dry to the touch and veinless, a pleasure to behold. This cigar weighs in at 54 x 110 (4.3"), a Petit Robusto.

I got nothing on the pre-light draw but could tell that it was going to be perfect. Once lit, I picked up leather with hints of wood. It started out as a medium to mild smoke. I could just detect a wisp of roasted nuts creeping in. The burn was good at the half-inch mark. At the first inch it was leather and wood with a little black tea. The ash fell on its own at about the first quarter and it turned out to be mild once my taste buds settled in. It was very easy to smoke, very smooth, unusual for a cigar this young.

Around the halfway mark this cigar had become very earthy with a touch of wood and spice...it was beginning to pick up strength. Into the third quarter the wrapper split open a bit but as I continued to smoke it opened up more. Although the cracked wrapper wasn't affecting the flavor of the cigar, it did make for one ugly and eventually uncomfortable smoke. It was turning a bit on me at around the last quarter but blowing it out would get rid of that nasty taste for a little while.

It was obviously a young cigar, and though they tend to smoke a bit rough, there was no evidence of it in this one. The cigar was a little busy and I felt it needed a bit of time to settle down. I think a few years down the road the first batch of these cigars that come out are going to be sought after by aficionados. That first release of an anticipated cigar is always the best and is rarely duplicated. I recommend buying them as soon as they come out if you have intentions of purchasing them.

—M.S.

# ✷ TRINIDAD SHORT ROBUSTO T EDICION ✷ LIMITADA 2010

Here I am trying this Trinidad once again. It's been almost two years since the last time I smoked one of these cigars and it hasn't changed that much. This particular one was gifted to me and so I wanted to see if it was any different than the box I have (or what's left of it). I have to say, I really didn't like this cigar when I tried it previously, it's not the style (flavor wise) of cigar I like. I know a lot of guys who love this cigar but unless it changes somewhat in the next few years I'm going to maintain my opinion on what I think of it.

These are darker cigars and this one was no different, the ones I've seen have all been the same. This one was hard to the touch and a little veiny. The pre-light draw gave me big cedar. Once lit, as before, very strong from the start with a lot of earth flavors. It was a bit rough at the beginning but smoothed out after the first quarter-inch and remained strong. Burning hot through the middle and had to do a relight—I hadn't reached the first inch yet. I picked up a hint of floral notes at about the three-quarter-inch mark and a few more times throughout the rest of the smoke. I have to say, from what I remember, it was a bit smoother than the one I smoked two years ago (and before that) but it still has a long way to go. I couldn't leave the cigar for a moment or it would go out. It seemed to be a little loosely rolled (even though the cigar was hard) and was consistently burning hotter through middle which made it go out, often. I found myself constantly touching it up with my torch. The flavors, once settled after the first half-inch, didn't really change much and all the relights didn't seem to change the flavor.

Even though they're a little better, I still have to say I don't like these cigars. I'm sure there are a few of you that will argue with me but there's nothing to argue about. We all have our tastes and this cigar is not for me. In my opinion, it still needs time but I don't think that's going to help the burn issues. I myself don't like to fight with a cigar and those of you who know me know that I've thrown many a cigar away almost as soon as I've started it because of issues. I don't like to waste my time with a bad cigar, life is too short. I did want to get through as much of this cigar as I could stand but in the end I let it go when there was about a third of it left. I really did want to like this cigar. I'll hold on to the couple I have left and probably wait a couple of more years before trying another. They still have a lot of life left in them.

—M.S.

VEGAS
ROBAINA

HABANA CUBA

ESTE PRODUCTO
PUEDE SER DAÑINO
PARA SU SALUD Y
CREA ADICCION.

MINSAP

REPUBLICA DE CUBA

Habanos

# VEGAS ROBAINA

## STRENGTH: MODERATE TO FULL

This brand, introduced in 1997, is named in honor of the legendary Alejandro Robaina, who was renowned by cigar aficionados around the world as one of the best tobacco farmers in the famed Vuelta Abajo region of Cuba. The Robaina family has farmed tobacco on their Vuelta Abajo fields since 1845. Don Alejandro, the senior member of this family, became a celebrity, with many cigar aficionados and tourists beating a path to his farm in the San Luis region of the Vuelta Abajo. Sadly, Don Alejandro succumbed to cancer in 2010.

Each year, 80 percent of Don Alejandro's tobacco harvest was deemed fit for use as wrapper leaf for Cuban cigars. Only 35 percent made the grade from competing farms. Today, Vegas Robaina produces a line of medium to full-bodied cigars that are exclusively handmade. The brand has quickly become popular among cigar aficionados.

## CIGARS

- Don Alejandro
- Famosos
- Únicos

# ✷ ROBAINA ART EDITION 2006 ✷

They call this cigar the Famoso Ramirez (Angel Ramirez is the artist who did the artwork on the band); it's a Hermoso No.4 or a Corona Extra. It weighs in at 48 x 127 (5"). They were packaged in numbered dress boxes of 25 cigars, only 200 were made and released in 2006. They have a double band, one being the Robaina and the other the artist's work with a number on the back. This is the first Habanos Art Edition done by Angel Ramirez, a very shy and talented artist that I had the pleasure of meeting years ago. As well as designing the band, he also produced four limited edition artworks.

The pre-light gave me wood and chocolate. Once lit, the draw was flawless, mild, with flavors of wood and straw. The construction on this cigar was superb; it looked like they put attention to the rolling of these cigars. About a quarter of the way through the cigar, the flavors hadn't changed, very smooth but still mild. The burn was good.

Halfway through the cigar, the ash fell on its own and the burn was perfect. This is a very mild and nondescript cigar but not unpleasant. A touch of earth crept in for a couple of draws but otherwise it remained the same throughout. I was able to smoke it down to the end.

I don't know how many aficionados would like this cigar for the hefty price tag that I imagine it has due to its exclusivity and that it doesn't punch you in the taste buds but I enjoyed it regardless. Especially since I knew both the cigar's namesake and the artist who designed the band. Worth a try, at least once.

—M.S.

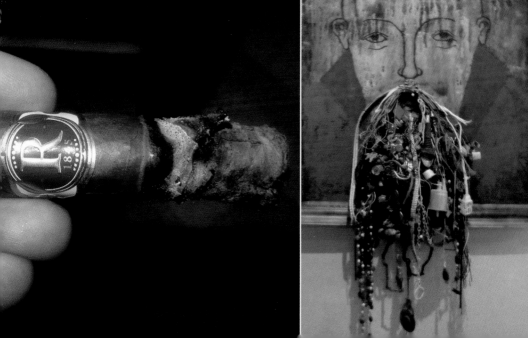

# ✳ ROBAINA PETIT ROBUSTO EDICION REGIONAL ✳ FRANCIA 2010

This cigar weighs in at 50 x 102 (4") but didn't make its 2010 release. Instead, 3,500 numbered, varnished, slide boxes of ten cigars each were released about two years later.

The cigar I smoked on this day was gifted to me by a friend. It was a little bumpy but otherwise smooth and as hard as a rock. I'm always worried about the draw when Cuban cigars are like this before lighting them. However, upon cutting the bumpy cap I took a pre-light draw and it appeared to be just fine and tasted a bit on the sweet side. Once lit and after taking a few draws, the burn was off. The start of this cigar was mild with wood and straw flavors. The draw was perfect and it tasted creamy at about the three-quarter-inch mark. A little further into this cigar and the cream is gone, being replaced by earth...yeah, what a change-up, more earth than wood. The burn seemed to straighten out only to go off again past the first inch.

Nearing the half I touched up the cigar with my torch and shortly after that the ash fell on its own. It's all earth now and still mild. I had to continually touch up this cigar, I couldn't stand to leave it alone to burn that way, sometimes affecting the flavor. I was able to smoke it pretty much to the end. It didn't start becoming harsh until into the last quarter.

I liked it even though it was a little mild. The flavors were uncomplicated and pleasant. If I was offered to buy this cigar, I would take a box of ten for sure (anyone selling any?). Especially good for people just getting into Cuban cigars, I'm sure it's not too expensive either.

—M.S.

# VEGUEROS

## STRENGTH: MODERATE

Vegueros has much in common with Cohiba and Trinidad, in that Vegueros existed as a mystery brand for a long time. The Francisco Donatién Factory in the Pinar del Río Province of Cuba began making cigars for the domestic market in 1961, and had been producing cigarettes in the years before.

The cigars rolled at the factory were mostly used for national banquets and public affairs. They became known simply as Vegueros. The name Vegueros refer to the farmers and field hands that work on Cuba's tobacco and sugar cane plantations. The style of the product resembled the cigars the farmers of the Vuelta Abajo region had fashioned for themselves for years—a handmade, rustic, and simple cigar.

Tourists who went on trips through Cuba's cigar tobacco-growing regions became familiar with the cigars. Habanos S.A. eventually launched the cigar brand for foreign markets in 1997.

In keeping with the Vegueros tradition, all the cigars produced under this brand are rolled by hand.

## CIGARS

- Entretiempos
- Mananitas
- Tapados

# VEGUEROS

EL ........, CUBA

16 Entretiempos

ESTE PRODUCTO
PUEDE SER DAÑINO
PARA SU SALUD Y
CREA ADICCION.
MINSAP

# ⭐ VEGUEROS TAPADOS ⭐

These cigars were not very popular for a time, but once they discontinued the line for a year and talked about a change and repackaging, all of a sudden everyone was interested in them (myself included). The Vegueros line started in 1997 with four vitolas and was discontinued in 2012. It didn't really sell too well. They were on the stronger side back then (a little too rough for my tastes); the newer ones are made on the milder to medium range. They're all sold in either cardboard packs of three or in a metal tin of sixteen cigars. The ones I purchased were a three-pack of the Tapados, which weigh in at 46 x 120 (4.7"). I don't know when it was packaged but they had just been released maybe only several weeks before, September, October 2014.

All three of these cigars were rolled exceptionally well. All as hard as a rock but once clipped and lit they all had a perfect draw. Smooth wrapper, light colored, few if any imperfections. It was just a really good-looking cigar that happened to have a Vegueros band on it. Priced a little cheaper, I really wasn't expecting much from it but there it was.

Upon first light, the draw was great and the burn was spot-on, well into the smoke. It was big on wood with a bit of creaminess to it. A quarter of the way through a little earth began to creep in. Near the half I flicked the ash (smoking indoors) otherwise it could have held on. The flavors hardly changed, and this was a mild- to medium-bodied smoke.

Past the half, this was still an easy cigar to smoke, still quite smooth. The burn began to be a bit off at this point but certainly did not affect the flavor. It began to pick up strength through the last quarter. I stopped when it became difficult to hold.

Excellent for what it was. The construction was better than some of the more expensive cigars. There is definitely a time in the day for this cigar. Will always have some with me in my travel humidor. You have to try them, do what I did, and buy a three-pack of the vitola you like. The other two vitolas are the Petit Robusto and the Petit Pyramide.

—M.S.

# CARNAVAL

## HABANA

# INDIVIDUAL CONTRIBUTORS

## MATTEO SPERANZA

Matteo Speranza is one of North America's leading authorities on Cuban cigars and lifestyle. He is a former hospitality industry veteran. However over the last 13 years he' been transitioning to the travel industry. He has made more than 30 trips to Cuba, exploring the cigar, food, and spirits industries in the country, traveling there for 4-6 weeks at a time, two to four times a year. He has fallen in love with the people and their customs while following his passion for cigars. He has visited the World Renowned tobacco farms of Pinar del Rio as well as numerous lesser known ones in the area, numerous cigar factories, and met many of the industry's luminaries along the way. He is also the author/editor of the highly acclaimed industry blog Cuban Cigars, Culture & Lifestyle. He has also been a guest writer on other blogs and cigar websites. He is currently planning a touring group for the cigar industry in Cuba. He currently lives in Toronto, Canada.

## CARLO DEVITO

Carlo DeVito is a lifelong publishing executive with more than twenty years of experience. He is a nationally recognized editor of food, wines, beers, ciders, and spirits. He has published Kevin Zraly, Matt Kramer, Oz Clarke, Tom Stevenson, Clay Reynolds, James Meehan, Salvatore Calabrese, Paul Knorr, Joshua M. Bernstein, and Stephen Beaumont, as well as Gordon Ramsey and the Beekman Boys. He has written more than fifteen books, publishes a highly-acclaimed wine blog, written for numerous magazines, appeared on television and radio more than one hundred times, and is owner of the Hudson-Chatham Winery. His recent books include *Life by the Glass: A Wine Lover's Journal*; *How To Host a Beer Tasting Party In Your Own Home: A Complete Kit*; *Mrs. Lee's Rose Garden*; and *Inventing Scrooge*.

## GARY KORB — "HOW TO SPOT FAKE CUBAN CIGARS" (PUBLISHED MAY 2014, CIGAR ADVISOR)

Gary Korb has been writing and editing content for CigarAdvisor.com since its debut in 2008. An avid cigar smoker for more than thirty years, during the past twelve years he has worked on the marketing side of the premium cigar business as a senior copywriter, blogger, and cigar reviewer.

## DENIS K. TOULOUSE — "CIGARS 101: CHOOSING YOUR FIRST HUMIDOR" (PUBLISHED APRIL 2013)

Denis K. Toulouse founded the blog Cigar Reviews at *Cigar Inspector* in 2007 in order to keep track of his cigar experiences. Based in Europe, Denis K. (as he is more widely known) has access to a wide selection of Cuban cigars.

## WALT WHITE — "THE BURNING QUESTION: BURN ISSUES IN CIGARS" (PUBLISHED 2011, STOGIE REVIEW)

Walt White is one of the cofounders of Stogie Review, a premiere cigar review blog. He can be found on any number of online cigar forums and is constantly pushing the limits of web technology.

# HANDBOOK INDEX

# CIGAR INDEX

HOLIDAY ISLES
OF THE TROPICS

CUBA

# ACKNOWLEDGMENTS

The publisher would like to thank Habanos S.A. and Cubatabaco for their support and cooperation. We would also like to thank Denis K. of CigarInspector.com; Gary Korb of famous-smoke.com and cigaradvisor.com; Walt White; and David "Doc" Diaz, Ed.D., Publisher and Editor of Stogie Fresh Cigar Publications; and of course, EffortlessGent.com. Also, thanks to Georgia Zola and Tatiana Laracuente of the Library of Congress for their help and guidance. And of course, thank you Whitney Cookman for the beautiful and elegant cover design.

I would like to thank my Cuban family and friends who have shown me a Cuba I would otherwise never have been able to experience. My good friend Amir who is always there to lend a helping hand which I very much appreciate. I am also appreciative of the many Cuban cigar industry insiders who have been kind enough to open their doors to an enthusiast such as myself. A special thank you to the staff at the Hotel Comodoro Cigar Shop who are not just friends but have made it understood that their shop is my home. And I can't forget the Partagas Cigar Shop family who I've known since my first trip into Havana and who consider me part of the family. Also, to Carlo DeVito who approached me to participate in this project. Alex Lewis, Brittany Wason and Jaime Christopher from Cider Mill Press who were a tremendous help and let's not forget John Whalen, the Publisher, without him none of this would have been possible. Thank you.

—Matteo Speranza

# CREDITS

Photos courtesy of Library of Congress. Copyright © 2016 Library of Congress. All rights reserved. p. 8, 9, 11, 12, 13, 14, 32-33, 41 (three B&W), 58 (B&W – bottom), 76, 77, 78 (top left; middle left), 82-83, 90-91, 92-93, 95, 98, 123, 124, 125, 129, 134 (B&W, top), 137, 140-141, 144-145, 290, 291, 296.

Photos used under official license from Shutterstock.com. Copyright © 2016 Shutterstock. All rights reserved. p. 2, 6-7, 16, 18, 20-21, 22-23, 26, 28-29, 31, 38-39, 41 (color only), 44-45, 48-49, 50,51, 53, 54, 55, 56-57, 58 (color only – top), 59, 60-61, 102-103, 105, 106, 107, 108, 109, 110-111, 116, 126-127, 128, 130, 142, 143, 146-147, 148-149, 156, 176, 228-229, 240-241, 260, 268-269, 300-301, 302.

Photos courtesy of Matteo Speranza. Copyright © 2016 Matteo Speranza. All rights reserved. p. 34, 36, 47, 67, 70, 71, 72, 75, 78, (top right, middle right, all bottom), 81, 96-97, 101, 150, 151, 152, 153, 154, 155, 159, 160, 161, 162, 166, 167, 168, 170, 171, 172, 173, 174, 175, 177, 178, 179, 181, 182, 185, 186, 187, 188, 190, 191, 192, 193, 194, 195, 197, 198, 199, 201, 202, 203, 205, 206, 207, 211, 213, 214, 216, 220-221, 222, 223, 224, 225, 227, 230-231, 232, 235, 236, 237, 238, 242, 243, 245, 246, 247, 248, 250, 251, 253, 254, 255, 256, 257, 259, 262, 263, 264, 265, 266, 267, 270, 271, 272, 273, 274, 275, 276, 279, 280, 281, 283, 284, 286, 287, 289.

Photo Courtesy of Mark Wilchinsky. Copyright © Mark Wilchinsky 2016. All Rights Reserved. P. 19

Map courtesy of Habanos S.A. Copyright © 2016. All rights reserved. P. 52.

Photos courtesy of www.CigarInspector.com. Copyright © 2016 www.CigarInspector.com. All rights reserved. P. 112, 113, 117, 119, and 121.

Photo of Ernest Hemingway Collection courtesy of John F. Kennedy Presidential Library and Museum, Boston. Copyright © 2016. All rights reserved. p. 138.

Photos courtesy of Havana Club. Copyright © 2016 All rights reserved. p. 131 (bottom), 132 (middle), 133 (top), 136

Photo courtesy of Ron Edmundo. Copyright © 2016. All rights reserved. p. 131 and 132 (top)

Photo courtesy of Ron Veradero. Copyright © 2016. All rights reserved. p. 132 (bottom)

Photo courtesy of Ron Cubay. Copyright © 2016. All rights reserved. p. 133 (middle)

Photo courtesy of Ron Mulata. Copyright © 2016. All rights reserved. p. 133 (bottom)

Photo courtesy of Ron Santiago. Copyright © 2016. All rights reserved. p. 134 (top)

Photo courtesy of Ron Vigia. Copyright © 2016. All rights reserved. p. 134 (bottom)

Photo courtesy of Sancti Spiritus. Copyright © 2016. All rights reserved. p. 135 (top and middle)

Photo courtesy of La Compagnie Des Indes. Copyright © 2016. All rights reserved. p. 135 (bottom)

Photos courtesy of Wikimedia Commons. p. 24, 30, 40, 43, 84-85, 87, 88, 104, 209.

Maps, tables, graphs courtesy of Wikimedia Commons: p. 40, 52, 62, 63, 64, 65.

# RECOMMENDED CUBAN CIGAR WEBSITES FOR FURTHER READING

Cigar Advisor
https://www.famous-smoke.com/
cigaradvisor/

Cigar Aficionado
http://www.cigaraficonado.com

Cigar Inspector
http://www.cigarinspector.com/

Cigar One
http://www.cigarone.com/

Cigar Press Magazine
http://www.cigarpress.com

Cigars of Cuba
https://www.cigars-of-cuba.com/

Cuban Cigar Website
http://www.cubancigarwebsite.
com/

Cuban Cigars, Culture & Lifestyle
http://www.
cubancigarsculturelifestyle.
blogspot.com

Finest Cuban Cigars
http://www.finestcubancigars.com/

Habanos S.A.
http://www.habanos.com/en/

Stogie Fresh Cigar Publications
http://www.stogiefresh.info/

YUL Cigars
http://www.yulcigars.blogspot.ca/

**For much more information
about authentic Cuban rums,
visit:**

The Master of Malt
http://www.masterofmalt.com

The Rum Diaries
https://rumdiariesblog.wordpress.
com

The Rum Dood
http://www.therumdood.com/

The Rum Howler Blog
http://www.therumhowlerblog.
com

The Whisky Exchange
http://www.thewhiskyexchange.
com